THE DOBERMANN

THIS IS the first full-length book on the Dobermann to be published in Britain.

The Dobermann is one of the most interesting of the modern breeds of dog. Its origin was in Germany and it has been evolved since 1880 from a number of breeds. In Britain the Dobermann is now classified in the Working Group of the Non-Sporting Breeds.

The first Dobermann registrations in England were made in 1909, but it was not until after World War II that enthusiasm was aroused and several of them were imported in 1947. The turning point of the breed really took place in the 1960s, and from that time onwards they have gone from strength to strength. There are estimated to be about 10,000 Dobermanns in Britain at the present time, and many of them are used as guard dogs, and a few as police dogs.

The author has a great knowledge of a number of breeds and she has now written a book which every Dobermann lover, whether owner, would-be owner, or breeder, will want to possess.

THE
DOBERMANN

BY

HILARY HARMAR

W. & G. FOYLE LTD
119–125 CHARING CROSS ROAD
LONDON, WC2 0EB

ISBN 0 7071 0490 4

© W. & G. Foyle Limited 1968
First published 1968
Reprinted 1970
Revised edition 1975
Reprinted 1976
Reprinted 1978
Reprinted 1979
Reprinted 1981
Reprinted 1982
Reprinted 1983

This book is dedicated to
Richard
and to all Dobermann lovers
and their dogs

Printed and bound in Great Britain
at The Pitman Press, Bath

AUTHOR'S PREFACE

THIS BOOK has been written to help the keen novice breeder of one of the most interesting dogs of the present day. The Dobermann is not only bred as a pet and show dog but also for police work and for use in war. These superb dogs are renowned for their courage, loyalty, swiftness and intelligence, which make them second to none. The owner of perhaps just one pet Dobermann should find useful information here, and who knows but that the pet owner of today may become the biggest and most successful breeder of tomorrow?

There are undoubtedly many ways of breeding, rearing and training Dobermanns, many of which are equally good. Breeders and pet owners will evolve the best methods to suit their particular way of life; but if any suggestions in this book are found to be of assistance, then the efforts put into it will have been more than worth while.

Dog breeders in general mean well for their particular breeds, but occasionally through ignorant breeding they allow faults to accumulate and end up by not being able to see the wood for the trees. Unfortunately, some breeds have suffered pathetically from this form of 'kennel blindness' which could perhaps be better called 'breed blindness'. This must not happen to the Dobermann.

My grateful thanks must go to the Kennel Club for their assistance, for the use of their library and for allowing me to print the Breed Standard; to all those people who so kindly lent me their beautiful photographs; to all those who have helped me in my quest, especially to Mr. Lionel Hamilton Renwick of the Birling prefix who was responsible for importing some excellent stock and who did so much winning in the show ring when the breed first started in Britain, and to Mr. A. B. Hogg of the renowned Triogen Kennels who helped with much detail and filled me with enthusiasm for this remarkable breed; to my long-suffering husband, who as usual not only corrected the manuscript but gave me moral support; and, last, but by no means least, to my daughter, Carolyn, who typed the manuscript, made many suggestions, organized the photographs and kept me up to the mark.

HILARY HARMAR

CONTENTS

CHAPTER 1

ORIGIN AND HISTORY

THE DOBERMANN, as we know the breed today, is of comparatively modern origin. It is also one of the few breeds of dog which have taken their name after the man who first originated the breed, Herr Louis Dobermann. The breed, however, did not in fact receive this name until five years after Herr Dobermann died in 1894. The breed was then called the Dobermann Pinscher and it has retained this original name since then, with minor deviations in various countries. Originally in Germany the breed was known as Thüringer Pinscher or Polizeilich Soldatenhund. In 1899 the breed was officially named the Dobermannpinscher (spelt in one word), and it kept this name until after World War II, when the word 'Pinscher' (meaning 'terrier') was dropped in 1949, as the breed was not considered to be a terrier.

In the U.S.A. the breed is still known as the Doberman Pinscher (Dobermann being spelt with one 'n'). This, too, is the name by which the dogs are known in Mexico, Central America and South America. In England, however, the breed is simply known as the Dobermann, which is spelt again with two 'n's in honour of the originator of the breed, Herr Louis Dobermann. In some ways it seems a pity that the dog should not have one name and one spelling throughout the world, as some breeders on both sides of the Atlantic get very upset if 'Pinscher' is added or omitted!

The Dobermann was unknown as a breed before 1865, although the foresters of Switzerland and southern Germany used a type of dog not dissimilar to the Dobermann. This type of dog was used particularly as a guard dog and for herding cattle.

Herr Louis Dobermann was a real countryman who was extremely fond of dogs, and he was particularly interested in breeding. He was born on the 2nd February 1823 in the little town of Apolda, Thüringen, which is situated in the southern central part of Germany. In those early days communications were bad, and the local inhabitants of the area made their own hobbies and pleasures. One of the interests of these country people was dogs and dog breeding, and Louis Dobermann was undoubtedly the leading light.

Herr Louis Dobermann held a number of jobs, which included being the municipal knacker, the local dog-catcher, and the official tax-collector. He was also the Administrator of the Chamber of Accounts, and at night he seems to have been the night police officer, and possibly at one time a night-watchman. Many of these jobs were extremely suitable for his pastime of dog breeding. As a knacker he could obtain cheap food for his dogs, and as the local dog-catcher he could probably acquire dogs that were suitable for his breeding purposes. For his night-watchman and police work he obviously required a good dog to accompany him on his rounds, and one of his first dogs was a dog called Schnupp, meaning 'Snuffler', a common name for many dogs in the area. For one reason or another, he never bred from this dog, as he had had him castrated before he was a year old. For some years it was impossible for Herr Dobermann to breed dogs himself, as until 1874 he lived in a small apartment. In 1880 he was able to move to a larger apartment, but there was still not sufficient room for dog breeding other than perhaps an odd litter. Finally Herr Dobermann was able to buy himself a small house and it was here that he eventually started his serious dog breeding.

The people of Apolda were obviously dog lovers and many of the inhabitants were keen dog breeders, and since the year 1860 there was a regular dog market there which was held annually. The object of this dog market, besides the buying and selling of dogs, was also to promote dog breeding. In this yearly show the dogs were all classified. There were hounds, butcher's dogs, guard dogs and little luxury dogs, and many others. In fact, the market was so big that there were generally at least one hundred dogs exhibited. Herr Dobermann was a regular visitor to this dog market, as it was here that he could view all the types of local dog. He was thus able to choose the dogs with the physique and character which particularly interested him. Herr

Dobermann, therefore, had the opportunity, not only as the local dog-catcher, to buy in suitable dogs to form the type of dog that he particularly wanted. This was apparently a large terrier-type dog which would be utterly fearless, highly intelligent, and a first-class guard dog. Luckily for Herr Dobermann, he had in the same town two enthusiastic friends who helped and co-operated with the breeding of his dogs. One was the grave-digger and the other was the church bell-ringer. One of his helpers, Herr Rebel, was also a night-watchman and he seems to have collaborated with the local shepherd, Herr Stegmann, who owned some parti-cularly large, strong and useful dogs, which he used for herding his cattle, and which he also took with him on his frequent visits to Switzerland, where he went to buy in new cattle. The route by which he travelled was by small, narrow roads and these were frequently dangerous not only from the elements but also from robbers. To make quite certain that his money was safe Herr Stegmann used to tie it to the collars of his dogs, because the robbers were less likely to attack the dogs than himself.

After a period of years the three men became renowned, with Herr Dobermann as their leader, for the fierce guard dogs which they bred. These dogs were in great demand and were sold as fast as they could breed them, fetching for those days a very good price, and their litters were large.

By the end of the nineteenth century, some years after Herr Dobermann and his two friends were dead, Herr Otto Göller, also of Apolda, started to take a keen interest in the breed, which was by then already established, and it is really he who took over the rough breed and commenced to improve it enormously. Herr Göller was quick to realize the use of the excellent brain and exceptional intelligence of the breed, its alertness and its excel-lent qualities as a guard dog. But he realized at the same time that the dog, as it was, was too fierce and vicious, and he there-fore set about taming the breed, in order to make it generally more amenable and useful. He was clever enough to be able to retain its superb guard-dog characteristics. He softened the breed so much that he even turned it into a good house-dog, and he eventually streamlined it so well that it became one of the most popular of all dogs in Germany.

Like all serious dog breeders, breeding with an aim other than purely financial, Herr Göller became utterly absorbed with his breeding, and it is really he whom the breeders of the present day have to thank for this superb dual-purpose dog. Unfortunately, Herr Göller found, as many other dog breeders have discovered to their cost, that many of his neighbours not unnaturally complained about the terrible noise that his dogs made, and eventually he had to send many of them away. This in itself was sad for Herr Göller, but it proved excellent for the breed, because other people bought the dogs and found them useful and highly trainable. Gradually the popularity of the breed grew all over Germany, and in 1910 the first Dobermannpinscher club was founded in Apolda by Herr Göller himself. Only one year later the breed was officially recognized in Germany.

The cult of dog showing became almost universal from the time that the first dog show was held in England in 1859, followed by the first show in Germany in Hamburg in 1863, and the first dog show held in the U.S.A. in 1874. It is interesting that the first stud book in Germany was produced in 1876 and the breed today can trace its history back to the Dobermannpinscherverein stud book of 1890. In 1899 there was only one colour recognized, and that was black and tan. In 1901 two other colours were permitted, namely, brown and tan, and blue and tan.

Unfortunately, the early breeders did not keep any records of their breeding, or, if they did, the records must have been thrown away or destroyed. It is therefore unfortunate that there are no real records of the early dogs that were used to make up the modern Dobermann. On this subject, since there is no proof, breeders have differing opinions, but there are certain breeds which have clearly been used to contribute to the present-day Dobermann, some of which have had a very strong influence.

There is obviously a great deal of the old smoothcoat, bobtailed German shepherd dog blood (not to be confused with the Alsatian which is only a little older than the Dobermann) and some strong influence from the old German Pinscher, now almost extinct. The latter is indicated particularly by the name 'Pinscher' being incorporated in the generic name. There is also considerable influence from the Manchester Terrier, which can be clearly seen in the great similarity in form and particularly in the markings and colour, both having the same rich rust-red markings. The Manchester is a great deal smaller than the Dobermann. It was originally bred in the area of Manchester in England, hence its name. It was originated from a terrier-whippet cross, and it was a dog much used for coursing rabbits. But they were perhaps most famous as being excellent ratters. The Manchester Terrier could, in fact, be described as a Miniature Dobermann, although Manchester Terrier breeders would probably prefer Dobermanns to be called Giant Manchester Terriers!

Another breed, which certainly had a very great influence and was one of the first breeds that were used, is the Rottweiler (meaning Village Pack). Its colour and markings are similar, and in the early days many of the Dobermanns produced the longer, thicker coat.

The Rottweiler was originally an ancient central European breed and it was used for centuries as a cattle-herding dog. Later it was used for hunting and was frequently kept in large packs by many of the German nobility. For a very long time they were known as the Rottweiler Metzgerhund (meaning Village Pack Butcher Dog) and so it was not surprising that the second name was dropped at the beginning of the century. The Rottweiler was also used for boar hunting and was probably descended from the Sauranger and Hatzrude (pack of hounds) and other Jagdhundrassen (hunting breeds).

Other breeds were incorporated in the make-up of the Dobermann, such as the old German Pointers, particularly the grey ones, the Weimaraner and the Vizsla Pointer of Hungary. One of the French breeds, probably the Beauceron, and the large blue Great Dane were probably used too, as also was the blue German Mastiff. There is strong evidence that the English Greyhound was used as well. In 1902 a Gordon Setter was introduced to improve the coat colour, but this it failed to do, and since the Setter coat is recessive to the smooth coat it still appears occasionaly. Sometime between 1900 and 1910 a very savage black Greyhound bitch was used. From the look and speed of the modern Dobermann it appears to have considerable Greyhound influence. There is a theory that there is some Dachshund blood in the breed, but this does not seem particularly likely since Dachshunds suffer from a hereditary malformation of the bones, known as achondroplasia. This is a congenital disease of the growing bones in which the cartilage does not develop correctly, and this results in the shortening and deformity of the leg bones. Other breeds which suffer from this are breeds like the Corgi, the Basset Hound and the Pekingese. It is interesting that it is caused by a dominant gene. The Dobermann shows no possible sign of any achondroplasia, and so the Dachshund theory can be dismissed.

The popularity of the Dobermann went from strength to strength and they were soon being exported all over the world. They are exceedingly good dogs in all climates, but they do not care for sudden changes of temperature. In 1904 they were sent to Holland, and from there they quickly reached the Dutch East Indies. Most of the European countries imported them, and in 1907 a number of Dobermanns went to Russia. In 1919 the Austrian Dobermannpinscher Club was formed. The popularity of the Dobermanns continued to spread and there were some in South Africa long before 1914.

In 1921 the Americans already had some excellent Dobermanns. Many of these were imported from Holland and later from Germany, Switzerland and Russia; and it was in this year that the American Doberman Pinscher Club was formed. The Americans did a great deal for the breed, as many of the original dogs had an aggressive and often vicious temperament. The Americans set to and calmed the breed, turning them into fine, useful, amenable and intelligent working dogs. There were four great dogs imported from Russia in 1930 which influenced the breed considerably.

The original German standard is of interest, because standards frequently become changed, not always to the benefit of the breed and often at the whims of strong-charactered officers of club committees or because the breeders cannot breed their dogs to the standard required. It then becomes easier to alter the standard than to alter the dog. In the original standard the qualities required were: 'Pleasant in manner and character, faithful, fearless, attentive and reliable watchdog, sure defender of the master, mistrustful of strangers, intelligent, gay, very capable of training, ideal house-dog and companion. Running gear must be light and free, temperament lively and ardent.' The size of the original Dobermannpinscher is interesting. Dogs were 58–65 cm. (23–26 inches) and bitches were 55–60 cm. (22–24 inches). In England the present-day standard is dogs 27 inches and bitches 25½ inches, and in the U.S.A. dogs 26–28 inches and bitches 24–26 inches, the heights preferred being dogs 27 inches and bitches 25½ inches, although it is rare to find dogs under 28 inches. This shows that the breed has increased in size considerably, and if this continues it may not be entirely to the benefit of the breed in the future. Measurement seems to be very elastic, since one never sees a Dobermann being measured in the show ring by a judge.

WAR DOGS

Dogs have been used in wars from the very earliest times, and many countries have employed them with enormous success. It was, however, the Germans who first officially recognized the tremendous value that dogs could have in war-time, and they developed their trained dogs from 1870 onwards. It is ironical that the Germans imported most of their original war dogs from Britain, and they encouraged village clubs, where people were to breed and train dogs. Matches were frequently held between clubs, and dogs became champions. By the time that the First World War broke out the Germans had 6,000 beautifully trained war dogs, and these alone saved more than 4,000 Germans, who would otherwise have died or have been taken prisoner. It was not until 1910 that the British started to train dogs. In the U.S.A., after they had come into World War I, an appeal was launched for 125,000 dogs. Special instructors were sent from England to the U.S.A. to train the Americans in war-dog training. France also had a very large dog-training organization. By World War II the Germans had 45,000 trained war dogs, and of these they sent 25,000 to Japan just before they attacked Pearl Harbour in 1941. In Britain there was practically no dog training done before 1910. In 1940, however, a special army war-dog training school was started, and this was sent to Belgium in 1945 with the British Army of the Rhine. Today the importance of war dogs is realized throughout the world.

The type of dog which is found most suitable for war is extremely interesting. Out of nearly 16,000 dogs that were offered for training in Germany in World War I only 18% were found suitable, and the top breeds were surprisingly the British Airedale and two German breeds, the Boxer and the Dobermann-pinscher, as they were then called. The Alsatian (German shepherd dog) came fifth.

POLICE DOGS

Although Dobermanns are used successfully as police dogs in a number of countries, it is interesting that in England the Police Force still favour the Alsatian to such an extent that they use about 99% of this breed, as they are easier to train. In 1967 there were 1,100 dogs in the English Police Force, of which only twelve were Dobermanns.

RECENT HISTORY

Just after World War II there were comparatively few Dobermanns to be seen in Germany and Holland. For some years the Germans were on a near-starvation diet, and many of the war dogs, like the horses, were taken over by the occupying powers.

In 1946 my husband was with the British mission to the Soviet forces in Germany and we frequently travelled round the area of Apolda, but we did not actually see any Dobermanns there. We did, however, see some in the East Zone in Leipzig and some in the West Zone in Hamburg. Switzerland, however, being a neutral country during the war, had retained some excellent dogs, and some of these were later imported into Britain.

Although the first Dobermanns were registered in England as early as in 1909, the breed did not for a long time become popular at all. The first dogs were not imported for serious breeding until 1947, when Mr. Lionel Hamilton Renwick of the Birling prefix, now so well known for his Miniature Pinschers, and Mr. and Mrs. Fred Curnow of the famous Tavey prefix, imported stock. Mr. Hamilton Renwick, who is also a famous artist of horses, imported a black-and-tan bitch, Britta von de Heerhof, and a dog, Bruno von Ehrgarten, and also a number of others which came from Switzerland, Holland, South Africa and the U.S.A. He had the honour of breeding the first champion dog. Challenge certificates were first granted in 1952.

Mr. and Mrs. Curnow bought their first stock from Germany. The dogs were Derb von Brunoberg and Beka von Brunoberg, and they were followed by others, imported from Holland and Germany. Later Mr. and Mrs. Curnow imported a great number of excellent dogs from the U.S.A. It has been their clever breeding for the past twenty years that has really put the Dobermann in the position that it maintains in Britain today. There are now a number of excellent Dobermann kennels in England.

British dogs are at present mainly American bred. In the early days many of the dogs were extremely vicious, so that they could not be shown in the show ring unless the handlers were standing at least ten yards apart. Otherwise fierce fights ensued. The first blending of the American and Continental blood in England did not have the desired effect temperamentally. Although the dogs were more elegant to look at, they were often very nervous. In the 1960s more American blood was imported and the breed improved greatly. It was then that the breed started to become popular. Now, with the clever selective breeding which has gone into the breed, the English Dobermann can hold its own against the world's best Dobermanns.

CHAPTER 2

INTERPRETATION OF THE BREED STANDARD AND HEREDITARY FAULTS

ONE OF the most interesting things about breed standards in general is that for years and years a standard remains the same, but over the same period of time breeds seem to change enormously. Looking at early twentieth-century paintings and photographs of Dobermanns and comparing them with those of Dobermanns of today provides an excellent example. The modern Dobermann is now a more elegant dog with cleaner-cut lines and a much more refined head than his predecessors. In the early days in the U.S.A. Dobermanns were exhibited in the Terrier Group. In England they are classified in the Working Group of the Non-Sporting Breeds.

The Dobermann standard is, on the whole, an excellent one. It was originally drawn up by men who were lovers of the breed, not only as working and guard dogs but also as show dogs.

As with all breed standards, the various breed points are often interpreted differently both by breeders and judges. What is required most is an overall correct type, soundness, and an ability to work well. A Dobermann should basically be a working dog, able not only to run fast but to jump and swim, and to have great powers of concentration; and last, but by no means least, he must have a good temperament.

The most important requirements in any breed are temperament and soundness in that order. A sound Dobermann means that he must at all times move and stand correctly on all four legs, be free from disease, defects and structural faults and be of good quality throughout. Having attained soundness, breeders can breed for other breed points, since the frills and minor alterations can be bred in comparatively easily.

The official British Dobermann standard is as follows:

18

CHARACTERISTICS. '*The Dobermann is a dog of good medium size with a well-set body, muscular and elegant. He has a proud carriage and a bold, alert temperament. His form is compact and tough and owing to his build capable of great speed. His gait is light and elastic. His eyes show intelligence and firmness of character, and he is loyal and obedient. Shyness or viciousness must be heavily penalized.*'

 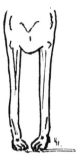 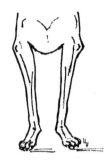

| *Correct.*
Fore legs
parallel. | *Incorrect.*
Narrow front,
'pigeon toed'. | *Incorrect.*
'Out at elbow',
cabriole legs,
weak pasterns. |

This is an excellent description. Since the first standard was made, however, the Dobermann has increased considerably in size, particularly in height. Consequently, he can hardly be called a 'good medium size', because a 27-inch dog (the American standard allows a 28-inch dog and some winning dogs are even 30-inches high) is really a large dog. Moreover, without splitting hairs over the size, the Dobermann is certainly what the general public consider a large dog. In Great Danes, the standard allows bitches to be 28 inches and dogs 30 inches high, and Great Danes are regarded as one of the largest breeds of dogs.

HEAD AND SKULL. '*Has to be proportionate to the body. It must be long, well filled under the eyes and clean cut. Its form seen from above and from the side must resemble a blunt wedge. The upper part of the head should be as flat as possible and free from wrinkle. The top of the skull should be flat with a slight stop, and the muzzle line extend parallel to the top lines of the skull. The cheeks must be flat and the lips tight. The nose should be solid black in black dogs, solid brown in brown dogs, and solid dark grey in blue dogs. Head out of balance in proportion to body, dish-faced, snipy or cheeky should be penalized.'*

The old Dobermann head was reminiscent of that of the Rottweiler, which was heavy and wide; but selective breeding has produced the clean-cut, wedge-shaped head of today's Dobermann. A wedge may be described as a slice from a round cake.

It is important that the wedge-shaped head should be enhanced by the 'parallels'. That is the top of the skull must be parallel to the line of the muzzle, and these two planes must slant slightly downwards forming a wedge with the line of the lower jaw. The line from the top of the nose to the lower jaw represents the blunt end of this wedge. The head viewed from above should form a similar wedge. Any form of snipyness and chinlessness causes the Dobermann to look weak. Hanging flews and any loose skin or dewlap immediately destroys the chiselled blunt ended wedge and the dog no longer looks strong, elegant and noble.

A strong jaw is essential for a working Dobermann. Many of the early twentieth-century Dobermanns excelled in jaw in comparison with some of the more modern dogs of today, and this is a point to be watched carefully. A long head often brings with it a weak lower jaw, and, as with many long-headed breeds, this is followed by missing premolar teeth. If the head is permitted to become elongated still further, then eventually more teeth would become missing. If the standard demanded a shorter head the tooth problem would be eliminated.

Care must be taken that in years to come the head does not become too narrow. The head should always be wide enough to encase plenty of brain. The length of the head should be in proportion to the rest of the dog.

If a breed is altered too quickly by reducing size or by enlarging the structure, it is found that the skin and bone do not alter in the equivalent ratio. In the short-nosed breeds, such as the Pekingese, the head has excessive folds of skin and wrinkle,

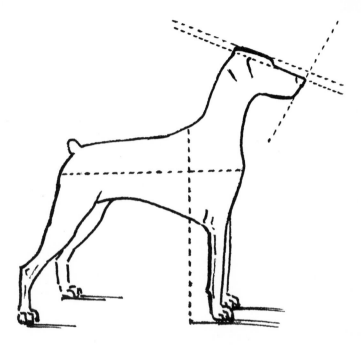

Diagram showing correct proportions of the Dobermann.

' . . . height measured vertically from the ground to the highest point of the withers, equalling the length measured horizontally, from the forechest to rear projection of upper thigh.'

'The top of the skull should be flat with a slight stop, and the muzzle line extend parallel to the top line of the skull.'

The head 'seen from above and from the side must resemble a blunt wedge.'

whilst in the long-headed breeds the ratio goes to the other extreme and the dog has a skin almost too tight for the skull. Nature works to rule, and woe betide any man who tampers with nature without knowledge.

The nostrils should be large and open. There should be a good reach of neck, as all dogs with great speed carry this feature. Many Dobermanns suffer from loose skin, which gives them too much dewlap and flews. This should be discouraged, as it is important that the Dobermann should be very clean-cut and that the skin should in general be tight like that of a Greyhound.

EYES. *'Should be almond-shaped, not round, moderately deep set, not prominent, with vigorous, energetic expression. Iris of uniform colour, ranging from medium to darkest brown in black dogs, the darker shade being the more desirable. In browns or blues the colour of the iris should blend with that of the markings, but not be of lighter hue than that of the markings. Light eyes in black dogs to be discouraged.'*

Correct eyes are extremely important, as they are the focal point of a dog. A Dobermann should be neither chink-eyed nor pop-eyed, and there should be no visible haw. For show purposes most people prefer a dark-eyed dog. Dark eyes certainly look smarter, but it is an interesting fact that all wild varieties of the dog have light-coloured eyes and that working dogs with light eyes work better than their dark-eyed counterparts. The reason for this is probably related to the fact that their early ancestors largely depended on their sight and scent.

EARS. *'Should be small, neat and set high on the head. Erect or dropped, but erect preferred.'*

There are many Dobermanns with over-sized ears, and these hound-like ears should be bred out. Ears that are too long break the line of the throat and spoil the entire clean-cut look.

There is no doubt that dogs with erect ears look smarter and more alert than similar dogs with dropped ears. Erect-eared dogs seldom suffer from any form of ear trouble. Since erect ears are dominant characteristics of the dog family and all early dogs had erect ears, it would be an excellent idea for breeders to start breeding for this more attractive and sensible type of ear. It has been achieved by the Bull Terrier breeders in a comparatively short space of time. It would certainly constitute a great improvement to the breed, and such selective breeding would eliminate the barbaric practice of ear cropping, which is still performed in some countries.

Ear cropping was resorted to about a century ago, in order to prevent the ears from becoming torn in fights when some breeds were particularly vicious. Since viciousness has for the most part been bred out of the breed, there is no longer a valid reason for cropping the ears.

MOUTH. '*Should be very well developed, solid and strong, with a scissor bite. The incisors of the lower jaw must touch the inner face of the incisors of the upper jaw. Overshot or undershot mouths, badly arranged or decayed teeth to be penalized.*'

The teeth should be even, strong, and very white. There should be twenty teeth in the upper jaw and twenty-two in the lower jaw.

The Germans are quite definite in laying down that the Dobermann must have forty-two teeth and that it cannot win a major award without a complete set; but there are other faults which are probably more serious than a dog having less than forty-two teeth. There is a saying that a judge who makes an exhibition of counting teeth may be covering up his general lack of knowledge of the breed! A standard requiring a slightly shorter head would eliminate the tooth problem.

An undershot jaw is more serious and more common than an overshot jaw. The edge-to-edge bite, although not mentioned in the standard, is a fault since it diverges from the prescribed 'scissor bite'. But this is the least serious of the jaw faults of the mouth, because with the edge-to-edge bite the jaw bones are usually correct and it is just teeth that are out of alignment, whereas in the overshot and undershot jaws there is a serious skeletal fault in the jaws themselves.

NECK. *'Should be fairly long and lean, carried erect and with considerable nobility, slightly convex and proportionate to the whole shape of the dog. The region of the nape has to be muscular. Dewlap and loose skin are undesirable.'*

Any form of loose skin or dewlap certainly spoils the beautiful clean line of the Dobermann and should be avoided at all costs.

FOREQUARTERS. *'The shoulder-blade and upper arm should meet at an angle of 90 degrees. Relative length of shoulder and upper arm should be as one, excess length of upper arm being much less undesirable than excess length of shoulder-blade. The legs, seen from the front and side, are perfectly straight and parallel to each other from elbow to pastern, muscled and sinewy, with round bone proportionate to body structure. In a normal position and when gaiting, the elbow should lie close to the brisket.'*

The shoulders should be well laid back, in order to enable the dog to move freely and with ease. Only when the dog is standing should the fore legs be parallel to each other. When gaiting, the faster the dog moves the closer he will place his feet to a central longitudinal line for natural balance. This must never be confused with moving close. The feet should only just clear the ground but the pads should be visible from the rear.

The angle of the shoulder-blade given in the standard of 90 degrees constitutes a well laid-back shoulder and goes with a good reach of neck, a slight dip in front of the withers, rounded withers and slightly sloping pasterns. All this can be seen without touching the dog.

BODY. *'Should be square, height measured vertically from the ground to the highest point of the withers, equalling the length measured horizontally, from the forechest to rear projection of the upper thigh. The back should be short and firm with the topline sloping slightly from the withers to the croup, the female needing room to carry litters may be slightly longer to loin. The belly should be fairly well tucked up. Ribs should be deep and well-sprung, reaching to elbow. Long, weak or roach backs to be discouraged.'*

The 'square' described in the standard is rather misleading, especially to the novice. Breeds which are required to be 'square' have level toplines and all four legs are included in the square. But since the Dobermann is required to have a sloping topline his hindlegs have to be extended beyond the root of the tail, and therefore he cannot fit into a square. It is much easier for the novice to visualize the two equal measurements of withers to ground and forechest to upper thigh. Therefore, a dog which is 27 inches high requires to be 27 inches long.

The slope of the topline should only be slight, and should not be made by extending the hindlegs in an unnatural position. The depth of brisket is really more important than the width. If the ribs are barrel-shaped they will obviously upset the action of the forelegs. The 'fairly well tucked up' belly enhances the entire, clean-cut, elegant, flowing lines of the perfect Dobermann and gives it the impression of being capable of tremendous speed. However, a Dobermann must on no account resemble a Greyhound.

HINDQUARTERS. '*Should be parallel to each other and wide enough apart to fit in with a properly built body. The hip bone should fall away from the spinal column at an angle of about 30 degrees. Croup well filled out. The hindquarters should be well developed and muscular, with long bent stifle and their hocks turning neither in nor out. While the dog is at rest, hock to heel should be perpendicular to the ground.*'

The first sentence, of course, does not make sense. When the dog is standing, the hindlegs from the hocks downwards should be perpendicular to the ground and they should also be parallel to each other and reasonably wide apart. The faster the dog moves when gaiting, the nearer the pads are placed to a central longitudinal line. It is important that the hocks should be well let down. High hocks often go with straight stifles, just as a straight shoulder often goes with a short, stuffy neck. Judges should penalize dogs which stand with their hindlegs stretched too far out behind them. Handlers often place their dogs like this, in order to enchance the slope of the topline from the withers to the croup.

FEET. '*Fore-feet should be well arched, compact and cat-like, turning neither in nor out. All dew-claws to be removed. Long, flat deviating paws and weak pasterns should be penalized. Hind feet should be well arched, compact and cat-like, turning neither in nor out.*'

This is well described. A compact and cat-like foot is one that is rounded and well knuckled-up. The whole dog is balanced on the strength of the feet. Nevertheless, it is a known fact with dogs as with human sprinters that some of the fastest runners are flat-footed; but the whole appearance of the dog is spoilt with these dropped arches.

GAIT. '*Should be free, balanced and vigorous with good reach in the forequarters, and a driving power in the hindquarters. When trotting, there should be a strong rear action drive with rotary motion of hindquarters. Rear and front legs should be thrown neither in nor out. Back should remain strong and firm.*'

Gait is extremely important in the Dobermann, because he is a dog who has been built to gallop and, since he is one of the fastest dogs in the world, it is important that he should be able to gallop perfectly. This movement cannot, of course, be seen in the show ring.

The 'rotary motion of hindquarters' is another part of the standard which appears to be meaningless. There is no part of the hindquarters of any animal which would rotate in a circle. The perfect gait should really incorporate the entire co-ordinated movement of the whole dog. This is not strictly possible in a Dobermann as he does not possess his full tail, and the tail in an unmutilated dog acts as its rudder.

A slow trot will determine whether a dog is sound or not. Many Dobermanns do not show to advantage at the slow paces. Nevertheless, they should be able to maintain a level topline at all speeds. Any form of prancing is wasted effort. The hackney action that is often admired by ignorant onlookers is not correct in the Dobermann.

When a Dobermann is seen from the rear, the feet should be

lifted well up so that the complete pads can be seen. The power of movement comes entirely from the hindquarters. The hindlegs from the hocks downwards should remain parallel. Unfortunately, cow-hocks are a rather prevalent fault in the breed and are a great sign of weakness. However, they are sometimes due to lack of exercise. The forelegs should also be parallel to each other when the dog is seen from the front. If the shoulder and hip angulations are correct, the length of stride will be equal in both front and hind legs; and the stride also requires to be long and not high.

A very good way to test the correct movement of a dog is to powder his pads with talcum powder or chalk and to get him to trot across a polished floor. The larger tracks left will be those of the forefeet, and these should almost be covered by the imprints of the hind feet. This gives a wonderful indication of how bad the Dobermann is in movement, since any deviations from the correct movement will be imprinted on the floor. This is extraordinarily simple to do and very revealing.

TAIL. '*The tail should be docked at the first or second joint and should appear to be a continuation of the spine, without material drop.*'

Until breeders become more civilized, tail docking for the show ring must continue. But it is undoubtedly a barbaric practice. It is a known fact that a dog with a tail can move faster than one without, an every working Dobermann would be a better dog with his tail intact as nature intended. Furthermore, an adult dog which loses his tail for any reason has to re-learn to balance. The cult of docking the Dobermann's tail was introduced in the early days of the breed, because many of the puppies were born with natural bobtails. This was inherited from the German shepherd-dog ancestry (not the Alsatian). As more Manchester Terrier blood was infused, the colour was proportionately improved and the natural bobtails almost disappeared, particularly when Greyhound blood was introduced as well.

Since the Dobermann has been built for speed there is no good reason for docking his tail.

COAT. '*Should be smooth-haired, short, hard, thick and close lying. Invisible grey undercoat on neck permissible.*'

The undercoat is more pronounced on dogs than on bitches. It should not be so thick as to spoil the line of the neck. The coat should also be dense and glossy.

COLOUR. '*Colours allowed are definite black, brown or blue with rust-red markings. Markings must be sharply defined and appearing above each eye and on the muzzle, throat and fore-chest, and on all legs and feet, and below the tail. White markings of any kind are highly undesirable.*'

Colours must always be clear and the markings must be distinct.

WEIGHT AND SIZE. '*Ideal height at withers: males 27 inches; females 25½ inches. Considerable deviation from this ideal to be discouraged.*'

These sizes are excellent, as they are within the limits of natural dogs and therefore fewer structural faults are likely to accrue. Taller dogs should be penalized as the tendency is for dogs to become higher and higher, and this may lead to strength and proportions being lost. Long legs are recessive genes. No weight is given.

FAULTS. '*Shyness or viciousness must be heavily penalized. Head out of balance in proportion to body, dish-faced, snipy or cheeky should be penalized. Light eyes in black dogs to be discouraged. Overshot or undershot mouths, badly arranged or decayed teeth to be penalized. Dewlap and loose skin are undesirable. Long, weak or roach backs to be discouraged. White markings of any kind are highly undesirable.*'

Dogs with dewlap and loose skin, and with long, weak or roached backs, should not only be discouraged but they should not be bred from. There are enough good Dobermanns without having to resort to dogs with serious faults.

In the U.S.A. the Dobermann is known as the Doberman Pinscher (Dobermann being spelt with only one 'n'). In Germany the word 'Pinscher' was dropped in 1949. Since 'Pinscher' is the German word for 'Terrier', this word has also been omitted in England.

The official American Doberman Pinscher standard is not quite the same as the British Dobermann standard, and it is as follows:

OFFICIAL AMERICAN STANDARD
(Published by kind permission of the American Kennel Club)

GENERAL CONFORMATION AND APPEARANCE. The appearance is that of a dog of good middle size, with a body that is square, the height, measured vertically from the ground to the highest point of the withers, equalling the length, measured horizontally, from the forechest to the rear projection of the upper thigh. Height, at the withers, males 26 to 28 inches, ideal being about 27 inches; bitches 24 to 26 inches, ideal being about 25½ inches. Compactly built, muscular and powerful, built for great endurance and speed. Elegant in appearance, of proud carriage, reflecting great nobility and temperament. Energetic, watchful, determined, alert, fearless, loyal, and obedient. *Faults:* Coarseness. Fine Greyhound build. Undersized or oversized. *Disqualifying faults:* Shyness, viciousness. *Shyness*—A dog shall be judged fundamentally shy if, refusing to stand for examination, it shrinks away from the judge; if it fears an approach from the rear; if it shies at sudden and unusual noises to a marked degree. *Viciousness*—A dog that attacks or attempts to attack, either the judge or its handler, is definitely vicious. An aggressive or belligerent attitude toward other dogs shall not be deemed viciousness.

HEAD (shape, eyes, teeth, ears). *Shape*—Long and dry, resembling a blunt wedge, both frontal and profile views. When seen from the front, the head widens gradually toward the base of the ears in a practically unbroken line. Top of skull flat, turning with slight stop to bridge of muzzle, with muzzle line extending parallel to the top line of the skull. Cheeks flat and muscular. Lips lying close to jaws, and not dropping. Jaws full and powerful, well filled under the eyes. Nose, solid black in black dogs, dark brown in brown ones, and dark gray in blue ones. *Faults:* Head out of balance in proportion to body. Ram's, dishfaced, cheeky or snipy heads. *Eyes*—Almond-shaped, *not* prominent, with vigorous, energetic expression. Iris of uniform color, ranging from medium to darkest brown in black dogs, the darker shade being the more desirable. In reds or blues, the color of the iris should blend with that of the markings, but not be of a lighter hue than that of the markings. *Faults:* Slit eyes, glassy eyes. *Teeth*—Strongly developed and white. Lower incisors upright and touching inside of upper incisors—a true scissors bite. Forty-two teeth (twenty-two in lower jaw, twenty in upper jaw). Distemper teeth should not be penalized. *Disqualifying faults:* Overshot more than $\frac{3}{16}$ inch. Undershot more than $\frac{1}{8}$ inch. *Ears* —Well trimmed and carried erect. (In all states where ear trimming is prohibited or where dogs with cropped ears cannot be shown, the foregoing requirements are waived.) The upper attachment of the ears, when held erect, should be on a level with the top of the skull. *Neck*—Carried upright, well muscled and dry. Well arched, and with nape of neck widening gradually toward body. Length of neck proportioned to body and head.

BODY. *Back* short, firm, of sufficient width, and muscular at the loin, extending in a straight line from withers to the slightly rounded croup. *Withers* pronounced and forming the highest point of body. *Brisket* full and broad, reaching deep to the elbow. *Chest* broad and *forechest* well defined. *Spring of ribs* pronounced. *Belly* well tucked up, extending in a curbed line from chest. *Loins* wide and muscled. *Hips* broad in proportion to body, breadth of hips being approximately breadth of body at rib spring. *Tail* docked at approximately second joint, should appear to be the continuation of the spine without material drop.

FOREQUARTERS. *Shoulder-blade and upper arm* should meet at an angle of 90 degrees. Relative length of shoulder and upper arm should be as one to one, excess length of upper arm being much less undesirable than excess length of shoulder-blade. *Legs*, seen from the front and side, perfectly straight and parallel to each other from elbow to pastern; muscled and sinewy, with round, heavy bone. In normal position and when gaiting, the elbow should lie close to the brisket. *Pasterns* firm, with an almost perpendicular position to the ground. *Feet* well arched, compact, and catlike, turning neither in nor out.

HINDQUARTERS in balance with forequarters. *Upper shanks* long, wide and well muscled on both sides of thigh, with clearly defined stifle. *Hocks* while the dog is at rest: hock to heel should be perpendicular to the ground. *Upper shanks, lower shanks and hocks* parallel to each other, and wide enough apart to fit in with a properly built body. The *hipbone* should fall away from the spinal column at an angle of about 30 degrees. The *upper shank* should be at right angles to the hip bone. Croup well filled out. *Cat-feet*, as on front legs, turning neither in nor out.

GAIT. The gait should be free balanced and vigorous, with good reach in the forequarters and good driving power in the hindquarters. When trotting there should be a strong rear action drive, with rotary motion of hindquarters. Each rear leg should move in line with the foreleg on the same side. Rear and front legs should be thrown neither in nor out. Back should remain strong, firm, and level.

COAT, COLOR, MARKINGS. *Coat*, smooth-haired, short, hard, thick and close-lying. Invisible gray undercoat on neck permitted. *Allowed colors*, black, brown, or blue. *Markings*, rust red, sharply defined, and appearing above each eye, and on muzzle, throat and forechest, and on all legs and feet, and below tail. White on chest, not exceeding one-half square inch permissible.

The foregoing description is that of the ideal Doberman Pinscher. Any deviation from the above-described dog must be penalized in proportion to the extent of the deviation, and in accordance with the appended scale of points.

SCALE of POINTS

GENERAL CONFORMATION AND APPEARANCE		
Proportions	8	
Bone-substance	8	
Temperament – Expression – Nobility	8	
Condition	5	29
HEAD		
Shape	6	
Teeth	5	
Eyes	3	
Ears	1	15
NECK	3	3
BODY		
Backline – Withers – Loins – Tail placement	8	
Chest – Brisket – Rib spring – Tuck-up	8	
Shape and proportions	4	20
FOREQUARTERS		
Shoulders – Upper arms – Legs – Pasterns	5	
Angulation	4	
Paws	2	11
HINDQUARTERS		
Upper thigh – Stifle – Hocks	5	
Angulation	4	
Paws	2	11
GAIT	6	6
COAT-COLOR—MARKINGS	5	5
Total	100	100

Disqualifications: Shyness, viciousness. Overshot more than $\frac{3}{16}$ of an inch; undershot more than $\frac{1}{8}$ of an inch.

RECOGNITION OF HEREDITARY FAULTS

Some breeders are so proud of their dogs that they are unwilling to notice or admit any faults in their stock or to see similar faults in dogs of the breed in general. Even if they do notice a fault, they would rather pretend that it simply does not exist. This is a dangerous form of kennel blindness which could quickly ruin a breed over the years. It is only by the recognition of hereditary faults that a breeder can breed good, sound stock. There are plenty of really typical Dobermanns in existence, and only these should be bred.

The faults in the Dobermann which require particularly to be watched are temperament, constructional faults of weakness, weak lower jaws, straight stifles, cow-hocks, bad fronts and roach backs, etc. The round, light eye is incorrect for the standard, but is in no way a weakness to the dog. Far more serious is progressive retinal atrophy (night blindness) which has caused great havoc in some breeds, and entropian (ingrowing eyelashes). The two latter faults are exceedingly serious. At the moment they are not considered a breed weakness, but at the same time they are not unheard of. It is therefore of the utmost importance to the breed, since the Dobermann is one of the soundest of breeds, that they must be kept so. It is therefore imperative that breeders must breed with honesty and give honest advice to each other regarding known cases of entropion or progressive retinal atrophy; and it should go without saying that any of these dogs should not be used for breeding. It is comparatively easy to prevent a malformation starting, but once a serious hereditary fault occurs in a breed it becomes exceedingly difficult to breed it out.

HEREDITARY FAULTS

PATELLA LUXATION. This is the name given to the dislocation of the knee-cap, which is called the stifle joint in the dog. Dislocation is the separation of two parts of a bone joint. Unfortunately, it is not uncommon in a great number of pure-bred dogs, particularly the type of dislocation where the patella slips too far back. In severe cases the hock joint goes quite straight, and to compensate for this the joint above the foot becomes over-flexed. In very severe cases the joint becomes locked, which is painful. Dogs with this fault often move extremely well, but they cannot stand for long without the patella slipping out of position. It can be seen too when the dog stands on its hindlegs. It seldom shows before the age of six months and sometimes not until after a bitch has had several litters, or when a dog is growing old.

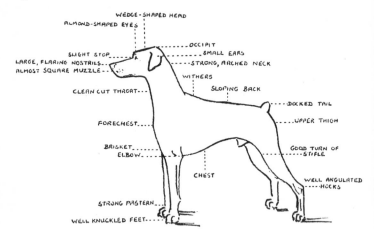

WEDGE-SHAPED HEAD
ALMOND-SHAPED EYES
OCCIPIT
SLIGHT STOP
SMALL EARS
LARGE, FLARING NOSTRILS
STRONG, ARCHED NECK
ALMOST SQUARE MUZZLE
WITHERS
CLEAN CUT THROAT
SLOPING BACK
DOCKED TAIL
FORECHEST
UPPER THIGH
BRISKET
GOOD TURN OF
ELBOW
STIFLE
CHEST
WELL ANGULATED HOCKS
STRONG PASTERN
WELL KNUCKLED FEET

POINTS OF THE DOBERMANN

A worse fault is when the dislocation occurs on one side, or occasionally on both sides to such an extent that the patella slips over the sides of the joint owing to the groove being too shallow. Again, this type of dislocation may not show before middle age or until a bitch has had several litters. This type of patella luxation is, of course, much more serious and can easily be seen when the dog walks. The dog will often give a sort of skip, and hop along on three legs for one or two paces, until the stifle has slipped back into the correct position. There is often the tell-tale click which can be heard, and the small bone at the joint can easily be felt with the fingers or the palm of the hand as it clicks in and out of position. Dogs with this type of patella luxation should never be bred from. The fault is rare in Dobermanns.

HIP DYSPLASIA. This condition is the name given to the abnormal development of the hip joint, and is a hereditary fault, occurring more frequently in the large breeds. The diagnosis requires an X-ray.

ENTROPION. This is a condition in which the eyelids turn inwards towards the eye and eyeball. Dogs with this fault should NOT be used for breeding. If the eyes are examined closely, the eyelashes will be seen not only to be growing inwards but to be actually coming in contact with the ball of the eye. This irritation starts off a discharge, and, if left untreated, ulceration of the eye follows and finally permanent damage to the sight. The fault must be treated by a small surgical operation for the relief of pain, but the dog most certainly should not be bred from.

PROGRESSIVE RETINAL ATROPHY. This is frequently known as P.R.A. and is often called night blindness, because the first signs of defective sight are generally noticed at night. It is a hereditary condition and extremely serious, so that it is important that no dogs with this affliction should ever be bred from. There are two types of P.R.A. In some breeds it has caused exceedingly serious breeding problems.

PROLONGED SOFT PALATE. This does not occur in the Dobermann. It occurs in short-nosed breeds, the flattened face producing a wide pharynx and a narrow larynx.

FAULTS OF THE MOUTH. *Undershot jaw.* This is the most common jaw fault in Dobermanns. It is when the lower jawbone protrudes beyond the upper jawbone. Dogs with this type of bite have an ugly, aggressive expression.

Overshot jaw. This is a bad fault, but it is not so common as the undershot jaw, of which it is the opposite—that is to say, the top front teeth protrude beyond the lower front teeth. Either type of mouth can be dangerous if a bitch should whelp on her own, as she may easily misbite the cord.

TEMPERAMENT. A bad temperament or viciousness are

generally hereditary faults. Although the majority of Dobermanns on the whole have good temperaments, viciousness is,
unfortunately, not unknown. There are occasionally to be found
puppies who are nervous or vicious, one fault often leading to
the other. This may occur from environment, incorrect handling,
a feeling of insecurity or from bad breeding.

Vicious dogs should be avoided at all costs except by the
expert who has the time, experience and inclination to deal with

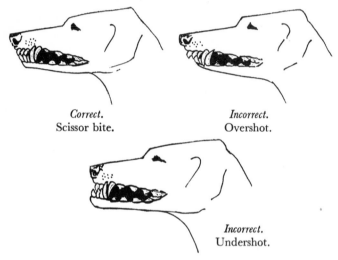

Correct.
Scissor bite.

Incorrect.
Overshot.

Incorrect.
Undershot.

such dogs. A vicious dog is nothing but a constant worry to his
owner and handler. It is far better to lavish care and attention on
a good-tempered, loving and charming dog. Tranquillizers can
help in the re-training of dogs who are nervous, but dogs of
uncertain temperament are neither good for breeding nor for
pets, and it is better to have them put to sleep.

One swallow does not make a summer, but, sadly, one vicious
Dobermann can give the breed a very bad name.

MISSING TEETH. This is a progressive hereditary fault, caused
by an over-elongated head. Dogs with less than forty-two teeth
should not be bred from, in order not to prejudice the continued
improvement of the breed.

Above: *Gin von Forell, U.D.*
German import.
Sire: German and Int.
Ch. Dirk Von Goldberg
Sch.H.III.
Owner: Mrs. M. Bastable.

Photo: Sally Anne Thompson.

Left: *A really superb head*
study of Vilja Germania
showing cropped ears.
German import.
Sire: Nigo Germania.
Owner: Mrs. M. Bastable.

Photo: Sally Anne Thompson.

Ch. Tumlow Impeccable (11 CCs.) and Ch. Tumlow Whinland's Flurry (6 CCs.).
They made Dobermann history by becoming champions when they won both the
Dog and the Bitch CC at three consecutive shows.
They were both sired by Ch. Acclamation of Tavey.
Impeccable was bred by Mrs. E. Harris (née Hoxey) and Mrs. J. Curnow.
Flurry was bred by Mrs. T. A. D. Hewan.
Owner: Mrs. E. Harris.
Photo: Sally Anne Thompson.

Gin von Forrell, U.D., at work.
Owner: Mrs. M. Bastable.
Photo: Sally Anne Thompson.

The superb Barrimilne Kennels.
Owner: Mrs. M. Bastable.   *Photo: Sally Anne Thompson.*

Twelve lovely puppies from a litter of thirteen bred and reared at the Triogen
Kennels.
Breeder: Mr. A. B. Hogg.   *Photo: F. W. Simms.*

Ch. Iceberg of Tavey. The Top winning Dobermann in this country. Best Dog of the
Year 1965 and Runner-up for this title in 1966. A multiple Best in Show winner.
Sire: Ch. Acclamation of Tavey.
Breeder: Miss E. Would.
Owner: Mrs. J. Curnow.   *Photo: Anne Cumbers.*

Celeste of Tavey at one year old.
Sire: Vanessa's Little Dictator of Tavey.
Breeder/Owner: Mrs. J. Curnow.

Photo: Anne Cumbers.

Ch. Tavey's Stormy Wrath.
A lovely bitch.
Sire: Ch. Acclamation of Tavey.
Breeders: Mrs. J. Curnow and Mrs. E. Harris (née Hoxey).
Owner: Mrs. J. Curnow.

Photo: Anne Cumbers.

Vanessa's Little Dictator of Tavey. A lovely American import who unfortunately may not be exhibited in England owing to his cropped ears. He is proving a very successful stud dog.
Owner: Mrs. J. Curnow.

Photo: Anne Cumbers.

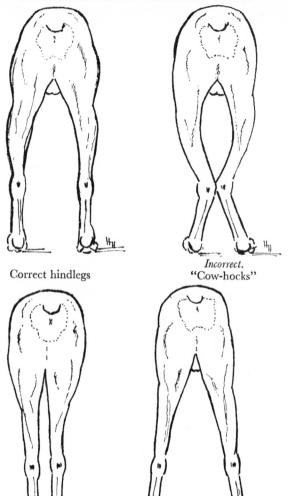

Correct hindlegs

Incorrect.
"Cow-hocks"

Incorrect.
Legs too close together.

Incorrect.
Legs too far apart,
straight hocks.

CHAPTER 3

CHOOSING, REARING AND TRAINING A PUPPY

THE CHOICE of a dog is always an important decision to make, particularly so when it is realized that the choice will affect the life of a family for a dozen years or so. Before the final decision of owning a Dobermann is made it is essential to consider carefully all the implications involved, particularly whether you have the right temperament to cope with a large, growing dog, enough time and energy to devote to giving the dog adequate exercise —this is important as he is a powerful, muscular dog—and enough money to be sure that the dog will be housed and fed correctly.

It is essential that the owner of a Dobermann should have the correct temperament to manage such an intelligent dog. This is a dog with tremendous character, enormous brain power, and exceptionally strong physique. The Dobermann will require exercise for his strong body, and strict training for his exceptional brain. Both of these require to be used to their full capacity. It is important too that the Dobermann from the very beginning should know exactly who is boss, and he must therefore at all times respect his owner. It should be realized that a Dobermann is certainly not suitable for anyone with a nervous temperament or a weak character. There is no doubt that a Dobermann is a superb dog and he will be at his best with someone who is by nature a dog lover, who is quiet, kind, resolute, firm, patient and, above all, consistent. The Dobermann is an exceedingly intelligent dog, and in fact he is always 'one jump ahead' of his owner. He is without doubt a dog for the connoisseur.

If there are children in the family, then it is important that both the children and the Dobermann should be trained to behave perfectly with each other. A Dobermann will not tolerate being teased. It is also extremely bad for a child to be permitted to tease any animal.

42

If the would-be owner of a Dobermann is sure that he possesses the necessary qualities and qualifications to own such a dog, then he should go ahead and buy a Dobermann puppy.

If the Dobermann is to be kept purely as a pet and is to live in the house as part of the family, then he is probably best kept in the kitchen during the early days, where he will do least damage to valuable furniture whilst still a young puppy. He must be house-trained and until then he should be confined to one room and not be permitted to roam around the house. He should also have his own bed and a place he can call his own. A Goddard or Safari bed is excellent, and a good place for this is probably under the kitchen table. But wherever the dog is to live, regular daily exercise is important, and when he is fully grown he will need at least two or three miles exercise a day. Running up and down a run is not enough for a large, energetic and intelligent dog, if he is to be well behaved and happy. He must be prevented from becoming bored, as this is when trouble starts. Sometimes dogs change homes several times, because their owners find them difficult. The dog is seldom at fault. It is generally the fault of the owner, who is not capable of looking after a large dog, so that the dog is not given sufficient exercise required to keep him fit, good-tempered and in hard condition. Even a six-month-old puppy will require three-quarters of an hour's exercise a day, and a nine-month-old puppy will require about an hour. If you are not prepared to spend the time on your dog and to exercise him adequately, it would be better to purchase a puppy of a smaller breed which is easier to manage.

WHERE TO BUY A DOBERMANN

When the family have finally decided that a Dobermann is really the most suitable type of dog for them, find out the nearest and best Dobermann kennels in the area. Most Dobermann breeders have their breed at heart, since they are not a particularly profitable breed. The Kennel Club will always suggest reliable breeders if you send a stamped addressed envelope to 1-4, Clarges Street, Piccadilly, London W.1, or 01-493 6651

There are also generally a number of advertisements in the dog papers. It is an excellent idea to go to a large show and look at all the Dobermanns and talk to the breeders. Arrange to visit a kennel, so that it is possible to see the parents and grandparents of the puppies. This is always most interesting; and if you are a potential breeder and should wish to show your puppy one day, you will obtain a good idea of what type of dog your puppy is likely to grow into.

CHOICE OF PUPPY

Choosing a Dobermann puppy of show quality before the age of seven or eight months is difficult. Never be persuaded to take a puppy before the age of eight to ten weeks. Puppies of eleven to twelve weeks should have had all the injections that they require, and at that age they are easily trained. Dobermanns will change homes without difficulty up to the age of six months to a year, but the younger they are the more easily they will settle down. After this age it depends largely on the temperament of the individual dog, and on the patience and character of his new owner. However, owing to the great cost of running on puppies most breeders prefer to part with them at eight or nine weeks. It would therefore be more difficult to buy a puppy of seven or eight months of age, and it would obviously be more expensive.

The puppy should look healthy and strong and be well covered. He should have a pliant elastic skin, sparkling oval-shaped, dark-coloured eyes, with a typical alert expression. There should be no haw showing. He should have strong, good, round bone, straight fore-legs, and well knuckled-up feet, a long, arched neck, a good, long, clean-cut head with a blunt muzzle and small ears, a good mouth, and a correctly placed tail. He should have strong hindquarters and a good topline. Most puppies, however, are inclined to be gawky in movement, particularly between the ages of three and seven months, so that this must be taken into consideration. A puppy should be friendly and should not cower in a corner at the sight of strangers, nor should he be aggressive. His coat should be thick and glossy, with no undercoat except on the neck. Attention should be paid to the colour, and particularly to the positioning of the rich, rust-red markings. The puppy should not be pot-bellied, as this is a sign of worms.

The mouth is correct when the top front teeth just overlap the bottom front teeth. The first teeth are always correct, but this is not always so with the permanent set. Slightly incorrect bites, however, often correct themselves, although mouths can change for better or worse. It is essential that a show Dobermann should have his full complement of forty-two teeth when adult.

Never buy a puppy simply because it has been advertised cheaply, as it may have some defect or a bad temperament. Find out the current prices for Dobermanns of good breeding; and explain to the breeder exactly the type of Dobermann required —a working dog, guard dog, pet or show dog, and whether for breeding—and the approximate price you are willing to pay. But do not forget that a good dog or bitch will cost a reasonably high price—probably in the vicinity of about £40 to £50.

PAPERS REQUIRED

Having chosen a puppy, the breeder will give you a diet sheet, which should be adhered to for a few days and then changed gradually as necessary. An inoculation certificate, a transfer form duly signed by the breeder, a registration form, and a receipt should be handed over with the pedigree.

AT HOME

On returning home with the new puppy do not succumb to the temptation of showing it off to all the family and friends immediately. Remember he is very young and has only just lost his mother, his play-fellows, and his brothers and sisters. His surroundings are strange, there are new noises, his bedding is different, everything smells strange, and his nose is very sensitive. He has probably been in a car for the first time in his life, and he may have been sick, in which case give him some glucose and warm milk. He may even refuse food for a few days, though this would be rare for most Dobermann puppies. If he refuses food, do not hand-feed him, but follow the breeder's instructions implicity. It is wise now to decide on his permanent name. Talk to him reassuringly, and in a quiet, gentle voice. If he is to be a house dog, let him sit on his bed beside you. Allow him to wander round and take his bearings. Let him come to you when he is ready, and do not fuss him and hug him. He will soon decide that you are his lord and master. If he has to be left for a time, it is probably safest to place his bed under the kitchen table well out of a draught. He will enjoy a tasty bone beside him, and, if possible, give him a small blanket or an old jersey smelling of you. This he will learn to love, and he will not feel so lonely when he is left alone. The loud ticking of a clock is both comforting and soporific, and so is a radio played quietly. See that he has a piece of newspaper lined with some strong plastic, where he can relieve himself if necessary. Remember his puddles can be very large and very frequent.

OUTDOOR KENNELS

If the Dobermann is to live outside, see that his quarters are dry and draught-proof. An excellent sleeping box for an adult dog is one which is made of wood, the dimensions of which should be 3 feet by 4 feet and 18 inches high, and the box should be raised off the ground about 6 inches. A small sleeping box to fit the puppy can be placed inside this main box while the puppy is small and changed from time to time to a larger box until he is fully grown. If the bed just fits the puppy he will learn not to soil his sleeping quarters. A large sack filled with clean wheat straw makes an excellent mattress. If the floor is of cement it can be covered with sawdust, which is easy to sweep up, or a thick newspaper can be put down where he is to relieve himself. Some puppies may take as long as a week before they settle down, but most of them settle much more quickly.

HOUSE-TRAINING

It is extremely easy to house-train a Dobermann on newspaper. Gradually move the paper towards the door near to wherever you wish him to learn to relieve himself. If this is to be the garden, move the paper nearer and nearer the door, until it is outside. By then he will know what is expected of him. From the very first days let him out into the garden every hour, gradually extending the time to every two hours, and then to every three hours. Put him outside immediately after each meal. Praise him when he has done what is required, and if there is an accident admonish him gently immediately, and make sure that he realizes he has sinned. Do not call him in the middle of the act in the wrong places as he will then undoubtedly waddle towards you leaving a large watery trail behind him!

HOW TO PICK UP A DOBERMANN PUPPY

It is important to learn how to pick up a Dobermann puppy correctly. He must never be picked up by the scruff of the neck, or, worse still, by the neck. Always lift the dog up gently with both hands, with one placed under his chest, the other supporting his hindquarters. Take great care not to poke a finger into his soft stomach. Later, when the puppy becomes larger and heavier, he can be held with one arm completely round his brisket at the top of the forelegs, with the other arm round his thighs. This can be quite tricky with a heavy wriggling puppy.

FEEDING

From the beginning the puppy must allow you to handle his food. He should never be teased, particularly over food, as any form of teasing will quickly make a dog bad-tempered and possessive over his meals. Feed all dogs separately at all times. To begin with, the new Dobermann puppy will probably be on four or five meals a day. The breeder will have told you what he has been eating, and you will be wise to follow this diet exactly for a few days before making new additions to his meals. The puppy at eight weeks should have a breakfast meal at about 8 a.m. This should consist of Farex or a cereal with about half a pint of warm milk with a little brown sugar or honey. Lunch should be given at about midday, and should consist of 6-8 oz. of finely chopped, cubed or minced meat, chicken, liver—care must be taken with liver as it is inclined to cause diarrhoea—fish (herrings are very nourishing, but beware of bones), ox heads, sheep heads, horsemeat, and when the puppies are older paunch and tripe are excellent. One of the prepared dog foods can be given occasionally. Red butcher's meat is the best of all and can be given raw. Most dogs prefer it this way, but dogs are all individuals and have their own preferences. Soak brown bread, rusks, or Laughing Dog puppy meal or some other meal in some tasty stock, and mix with the meat. The meal should not be too wet. Marmite is excellent for stock as it contains yeast. Grated cheese is much appreciated. At tea-time the puppy should have another meal of milk and cereal or puppy meal and a beaten-up egg yolk. It is better not to give the white of the egg. Dinner can consist of Weetabix with 6-8 oz. of meat, or plain puppy meal and gravy. Finally, last thing at night, at about 10 p.m., give him a final meal of Farex or Weetabix with milk, or just plain milk, which can be left down for the night, if there is any left! Laughing Dog Wheatmeal biscuits are always appreciated. A meal consisting of one-third Ful-o-Pep (made by Quaker Oats), one-third Lowe's Carta Carna and one-third meat provides an excellently balanced diet.

Once a day give either Abidec vitamins or halibut liver oil capsules, the quantity depending on the age. A puppy could have one capsule daily, gradually increasing this to three capsules a day when adult. This is excellent during the winter but not so important in the summer. Never leave food down on a plate for more than fifteen minutes except at night, because otherwise flies may settle on it and the puppy may pick up an infection. Butcher's meat can be fed raw, or cooked in a pressure cooker with vegetables, which makes excellent gravy. See that there is fresh water always at hand.

GUIDE TO FEEDING

A dog normally requires $\frac{1}{2}$–1 oz. of food per pound of body weight, depending on his age, amount of exercise he is getting, and the climate. From two to four months of age a Dobermann puppy requires four to five meals a day. From four to six months he requires three meals a day. From six months to a year he can manage on two meals a day, and from one year onwards one meal a day should be sufficient, except for bitches in whelp and for older dogs, who require two meals daily. As the number of meals is decreased, the quantity of food must be gradually increased. An adult dog requires 1–1$\frac{1}{2}$ lb. of meat and 1–1$\frac{1}{2}$ lb. of meal per day.

As with all fast-growing breeds, it is useful to give Collo-Cal D

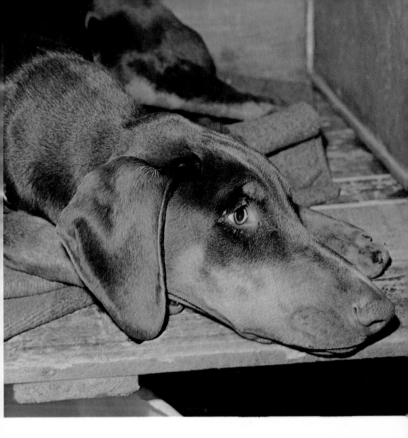

Brown Doberman on show bench

Colour photos by Anne Cumbers

Lunch for two hungry puppies, served in a non-chewable stainless steel dish

Seven week old Doberman puppies by Roanoke Double Diamond ex. Roanoke Ramona

Non-chewable metal bucket for drinking water, tied up to prevent puppies playing football with it

Roanoke Carol being trained to stand for show at an early age

Grooming with a leather glove

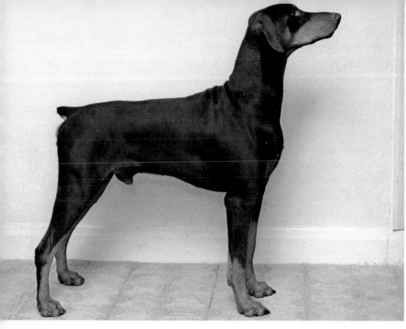

Twenty month old red and tan Doberman : Studbriar Cassius

Correct type of whelping box for a bitch and puppies

(high potency) which can be obtained from the vet, or some form of calcium with Vitamin A and D. At eight weeks a puppy requires one-eighth of a teaspoonful once a day. Increase gradually, so that at three months he is taking a quarter of a teaspoonful daily. Continue the dosage until the age of one year to eighteen months, depending on the size of the dog. The dose must *never* exceed a quarter of a teaspoonful daily. It would be wise to ask the vet's advice for your individual dog. Puppies make their maximum growth between three and nine months, and during these vital months correct feeding is of the utmost importance.

It is important that all dogs should have plenty of fresh water to drink. Be sure to get the water from the mains tap and never use water from the hot-water tap unless boiled. Always tip any water kept in the garden or dog runs away for the night, as a diseased rat using this water could cause a serious infection.

A good hard dog biscuit, such as Laughing Dog Wheatmeal, is excellent for the Dobermann to chew, and part of a block can be given each evening. Dogs will also enjoy a really large shinbone from the butcher's which keeps them occupied for hours.

Never give Dobermanns sloppy meals. It is important to give the dogs a variety of food. They love paunch when they are older, but it must be well washed and well cooked. Sheep's heart and organ meat lack calcium but they are nice for a change. Dogs also love dried kennel fish, but be sure to get the best quality. Since it is very salty, however, the dogs will require plenty of water to drink. Vetzyme, which is a Phillips product, is an excellent form of yeast. Halibut liver oil, in capsules, and calcium are both excellent additions to the diet. A teaspoonful of Crest Seaweed Powder or iodized salt is also good for them.

DIARRHOEA

A wise owner should keep a bottle of kaolin mixture in case of diarrhoea. If there is only a small amount of diarrhoea and the puppy seems well, give a dose of the mixture two or three times during the day. If, however, the diarrhoea should continue, stop all milk and milk-foods for at least twenty-four hours after the diarrhoea has ceased. Give plenty of water to drink and sweetened arrowroot added to diluted Protogest. The following day give a little boiled rice in gravy, and gradually return to a normal diet. If there should be blood in the stools, be sure to get the vet immediately, and see that the puppy has an antibiotic injection within the hour. This rapid action may well save the puppy's life, or keep it from having a prolonged illness. Yogurt is extremely good for all cases of diarrhoea.

EXERCISE

A young Dobermann puppy of four months can be taken for short walks, so that he may quickly become accustomed to a collar and lead. A suitable chain slip-collar is really essential for training. At six months a puppy requires about three-quarters of an hour's mixed exercise, both road work and off the lead in a field. A game with a ball gives the dog good exercise and saves the owner extra effort! Remember that all Dobermanns are apt to be headstrong as regards following a trail, and so keep the dog away from all roads when he is off a lead, until it is absolutely certain that he is under complete control.

A Dobermann is a dog of habit and he will remain content provided that he is given his expected daily exercise. In other words, he will be happier with a set amount of exercise daily rather than a ten-mile walk on Sundays and nothing during the week.

REST

The Dobermann puppy, like all young animals, requires plenty of rest interspersed with playful exercise and not too much excitement. If he is kept in kennels he does not require artificial heat provided that the kennels are dry and draught-proof. If the Dobermann is a house dog, he must not be allowed to get too near a fire as extremes of temperature are dangerous owing to the likelihood of catching a chill. If he is in the garden, he should have some protection from the sun and also from rain. If he gets wet he must be dried thoroughly, especially his feet and tummy.

INOCULATIONS

A puppy should be inoculated against distemper, virus

hepatitis, leptospira canicola and leptospira icterohaemorrhagiae between the ages of eleven and sixteen weeks, depending on the brand of the inoculation. It is a wise precaution to have a booster injection once a year.

WORMING

Puppies should be wormed at the age of five weeks, to prevent larvae from entering the body on their normal migration. This is particularly important with bitches, because if they are wormed when they are six weeks old they will not pass larvae on to their future puppies unless they become reinfested. A repeat worming should be done ten days later and again at six months, or whenever worms are suspected.

It is important to weigh each puppy before worming, as the dosage of worm powder given must be exact. In these days there is no necessity to starve a puppy before worming; but each puppy should be put separately after worming, so that the results, if any, can be seen. Puppies occasionally vomit up worms. Many of the new worm powders dissolve the worms and none may be seen. If, however, there are traces of them, collect them up carefully and either burn them or put them down the lavatory. Pull the plug immediately and disinfect the bowl. Be sure to wash your hands thoroughly afterwards.

Dobermanns, like all large dogs, are renowned for excellent teeth, but not necessarily good mouths. The milk teeth generally change normally and easily between four and four and a half months of age, and the permanent teeth are all through by the age of eight months. Occasionally, a puppy may require assistance in shedding his eye-teeth. These can be removed with tweezers as soon as they are loose. During the periods of teething, puppies should be given large shin-bones to chew. If something hard is not specifically provided, they will find something themselves, and it may be something of value to their owner.

SIZE AND WEIGHT

The size of puppies varies, dogs generally being larger than bitches. Adult dogs average 27 inches and bitches $25\frac{1}{2}$ inches, and their average weights are approximately 50–75 lb., although some Dobermanns weigh as much as 90 lb.

As a rough guide, puppies usually weigh between about 8 and 16 oz. at birth. However, the birth weight seldom bears any relation to the ultimate size of the dog. The bitches are generally heavier than the dogs until the age of five weeks. The following is a rough guide to the average weight of dog and bitch puppies:

At one week the bitches weigh 1 lb. 6 oz. and the dogs 1 lb. 5 oz.

At two weeks the bitches weigh 2 lb. 9 oz. and the dogs 2 lb. 7 oz.

At three weeks the bitches weigh 3 lb. 6 oz. and the dogs 3 lb. 4 oz.

At four weeks the bitches weigh 4 lb. 12 oz. and the dogs 4 lb. 8 oz.

At six weeks dogs take over and are about 2 oz. heavier than the bitches. Dogs then weigh about 8 lb. 4 oz. and the bitches weigh 8 lb. 2 oz.

At eight weeks of age the difference is often as much as half a pound, dogs usually weighing about $12\frac{1}{2}$ lb. and bitches about 12 lb.

At twelve months Dobermanns are nearly fully grown; but they will fill out after that age.

The older dog puts on weight in bone, even if he does not actually become fatter. Bitches usually have their first season at seven months, although some come in season earlier and some later. A bitch should not be mated before her second season. By that age she should be fully developed and mentally mature enough to cope with a large litter.

TRAINING

A Dobermann requires to be taught discipline with kindness from his earliest days. There is probably no breed of dog who, when trained, will repay his owner with greater alertness, intelligence, courage, loyalty, obedience and utter fearlessness. He is also a splendid watchdog and he will guard his owner's life and his family and property to the bitter end. The Dobermann is also one of the fastest breeds of dog. He is a dog of enormous character and is excellent with children, only his size and strength being possible disadvantages. He does not like intruders and therefore makes an extremely good burglar alarm.

This great dog is a utility dog and he likes to work as his ancestors did. He is always happy when working and he is certainly a dog to be truly proud of.

If a Dobermann should ever show any form of viciousness or bad or uncertain temperament, then he should not be kept, as he will be nothing but a perpetual worry to his owner and his owner's family. Since there are numerous Dobermanns with excellent temperaments, a vicious one should be put to sleep.

A Dobermann puppy at three weeks is utterly amenable and can be trained with the greatest of ease to stand in a show pose. But as he gets older he will become more difficult as he gradually realizes his strength and his intelligence. By the time that he is seven to eight months old he will be embarking on his rebellious 'teenage' stage. This is the time that he requires his real training. From eight to twelve months of age he is in his most difficult period of all, since it is then that there is most likely to be a clash of wills, as he can become extremely stubborn. It is essential that he should know who is boss at this age, and his owner must therefore have adequate time to cope with his Dobermann. By the time that the dog is a year old it is essential that his master should be in complete command.

There are some excellent dog-training schools in the country, where a dog can be superbly trained. Unfortunately, in many cases, the owner does not know how to manage his trained dog, and when the dog comes home he soon senses that his owner does not know what is required of him. In a few days the dog is almost unmanageable again. It is therefore very much better for the dog and his owner to be trained at a local dog-training society. These societies are to be found all over the country, and the Kennel Club will always give the names of the nearest ones in a given area. It is best for the dog to start his lessons when he is about six months old. There is a great deal more pleasure in having trained one's own dog.

There is probably no more devoted, loyal, or intelligent dog than the trained Dobermann. He will be devoted to his family, and the family, without knowing it, will in actual fact be completely owned by their Dobermann!

HANDLING PUPPIES

Puppies should be accustomed to being handled and loved from birth. As soon as they are exactly three weeks old they should be given a particular amount of attention during the following week, as love at this time will effect them all their lives. It is most interesting to note that twenty-day-old puppies are hardly aware of their surroundings, and only warmth and hunger and sleep matter to them, whereas on the twenty-first day they become aware of their surroundings, of people, and of other animals, etc. It is almost as if they have been hatched from an egg. The fourth week will form the dog's basic character. Playing must be done quietly and gently, and much praise and encouragement must be given at all times.

Gradually the puppy should become accustomed to as many situations and noises as possible. He should also not resent being touched by strangers. He must become accustomed to car horns and any sudden noises. Metal tins filled with stones can be thrown about in a game. These kinds of antics all help to make him brave and fearless.

Dobermanns can only be trained with extreme kindness, gentleness, and, as with all animals, firmness is absolutely essential. *Never* smack a small puppy, particularly on its hindquarters or on the head. It only causes nervousness. They should be trained when they are really young. It is better to shake him by picking him up by the scruff of the neck. (This does not hurt him physically but his pride is hurt and so it is more effective than smacking.)

EARLY TRAINING

Training can start at the age of about twelve weeks. The Dobermann's first lessons must be getting used to having a collar round his neck. Use a very light one and put it on just before a meal, and he will then quickly forget that it is there. It is quite a good idea to have a short end attached to the collar so that other puppies pull it when playing, and the puppy quickly gets used to being pulled along by the collar as a game.

The best equipment for training puppies is a four- to six-foot webbed leash or a plain strong leather one. A chain slip-collar is absolutely essential. Choose one according to the size of the dog. At each end there is a large metal ring. It is imperative to learn to put the chain slip-collar on correctly. First, slip the chain through one ring; this forms the collar. Place the dog on your left side and slip the collar over the head so that the pull on the chain goes from left to right. This enables the collar to be tightened when the leash is pulled, and the collar loosens the moment the pressure on the leash is stopped. If the dog is on the right-hand side of the handler the collar like this will be incorrect. The leash must be slack all the time, except when the dog is being corrected.

The next stage is to put a lead on to a chain slip-collar just before a meal. Allow it first to hang a little so that the puppy gets used to the extra weight, and then gently pick the lead up. The dog must be on the handler's left-hand side. The left hand should hold the leash close to the collar, and the other end of the leash should be held in the right hand. All corrections are made by a quick firm jerk with the left hand. When starting to walk, always start off with the left foot. Take the puppy to an area it has never been in before. Pull the lead fairly sharply but gently, and immediately let it go loose again. Keeping the puppy walking to heel, say 'Heel!' as you go in a sharp tone. A rolled-up newspaper is useful to tap his nose when he walks too far in front, or an excellent method to prevent the dog walking in front of you is to turn completely round and walk in the opposite direction, giving a sharp jerk on the lead and commanding the dog to 'Heel!' As soon as the puppy is walking to heel correctly change the tone of voice and say 'Good boy!' Continue in the sharper tone—'Heel!', etc.

Some puppies are very quick at learning about walking on a lead and within a few minutes they will be trained, whilst others can be little devils; but patience is all that is required, with plenty of praise and reward. Jerk the lead and walk, jerk the lead again and walk, and continue until you have got the puppy doing what *you* want. *Never* stop until he has done what is required. Then give much praise and a titbit. Spend ten minutes on the training each day. But a word of warning: you may have trained a puppy very quickly, but never forget that without constant practice he can also forget extremely quickly. Once he has learnt, though, it will never take long to train him again.

The training of any large breed of dog is really important, as the enjoyment of owning a beautiful trained dog is well worth the initial effort. Being dragged along by an untrained dog is unpleasant in the extreme and very tiring, besides making the owner look the fool he is.

There are a few other elementary lessons that a Dobermann should be taught.

JUMPING UP ON PEOPLE. This is a very irritating habit and should be curbed while the puppy is young. Dirty muddy paws ruin clothes and sharp nails tear stockings. It is also a dangerous habit, particularly where old people and small children are concerned. Every time that a puppy jumps up, try to anticipate his action, saying 'No!' in a firm, severe voice, at the same time catching his paws and pushing him firmly down on to the ground, repeating 'No!' When the puppy obeys, pat him and in a honeyed voice say 'Good boy!' If, however, he persists in jumping up (and he surely will), then catch each of his forepaws, one in each hand, and squeeze the toes together just hard enough and sharply enough to make it hurt. Then let go quickly, and in the same firm voice say 'No!' and push him down. He will soon get the idea that jumping up hurts him. Another method is to step on his hind feet which will have the same effect. A young puppy may not perhaps do much damage while he is small by jumping up, but it is a different matter when he weighs between 75 and 90 lb.

BARKING. Senseless barking is annoying in the extreme. The Dobermann should be trained very early to bark only at the arrival of strangers, but he should stop immediately when told that the strangers are acceptable and that all is well with his owners and their home. One of the simplest methods to train a dog not to bark is to put him in a room on his own and when he starts to bark and howl, and he automatically will, go in and in a highly rating and commanding voice say 'No!', and when he takes no notice at all, and continues to bark, use a lightly folded-up newspaper or magazine and bang it hard on your hand, at the same time saying 'No!' in the crossest possible voice. Go out of the room, repeat the exercise by banging on the door and shouting 'No!' at the top of your voice, at the same time banging the newspaper. The puppy will quickly realize that barking is displeasing to his lord and master, and all puppies want to please. As soon as he is quiet, go in and pat him and perhaps even reward him with a titbit. It is important that he should never be permitted to bark except at the arrival of strangers. It is no good allowing him to bark for half an hour one day by merely turning up the television because you are too lazy to go out and rate him properly. Like all training, it must be consistent.

BITING. No dog should ever bite. If he ever goes for anyone viciously, he should be put to sleep immediately. The responsibility of owning a vicious dog is too great, because, if a dog did serious facial damage to a young child, or knocked an old person down, the owner would suffer from a guilty conscience for the rest of his life. It is better to put the dog to sleep than to wait for him to do something really serious.

GROWLING. This should not be permitted and the Dobermann must be made to understand this in no uncertain terms. From earliest puppyhood the dog must not be allowed to become possessive of his bed, or blanket, or a toy. If he has a bone never try to take it away from him, as this is not fair. It is a different matter when he growls and barks at the arrival of strangers.

SITTING ON CHAIRS. It is far better not to allow a large dog like a Dobermann to sit on chairs. He should be provided with his own bed or basket and he should be trained that when his owner shouts 'Bed!' he will get up and go to his own bed from wherever he is in the house or garden. To begin with he will have to be trained that it is a sin to sit on his master's sofas and chairs. Again, using the rolled-up-paper method, slap the rolled-up paper hard on the hand and say 'No!' or 'Get off!' in a harsh rating voice. The puppy will soon learn that he is only allowed to sit or lie on his own bed. On no account should a dog be permitted to sit on chairs sometimes and not at other times, as this is utterly confusing.

CHASING CARS. This is an extremely dangerous habit, and so it should be anticipated by training a puppy to beware of cars, and this requires the co-operation of someone else to drive the car. Walking with the dog on the lead, arrange for the car to go past, and as it does so the horn should be sounded loudly and sharply. At the same moment the handler should pull the dog sharply to one side with a jerk. Repeat the lesson a number of times and the dog will soon learn to be respectful of all passing traffic, and this must include buses, bicycles and motor-bicycles.

OBEDIENCE TRAINING

There is no better place for a novice to train his Dobermann than at his local obedience classes, and he can learn quite advanced training there. A Dobermann should never be trained for defensive tactics except by experts, such as the police and the Army Dog School, etc., as this training can lead to highly dangerous dogs in the wrong hands.

SHOW TRAINING

As soon as a young puppy can stand really upright and walk about on his own he can be trained to stand in a show pose. This can be done on a table, on a non-slippery surface, for the convenience of the handler. But when he is older a low table of about 18 inches off the ground makes a good platform. When he is small place him on the table so that his forelegs remain parallel to each other and the paws touch the table at the same time, and then slowly drop his hind feet into the correct position.

To correct his stance, start by placing the off foreleg in the desired position and then slide the hand over the dog without losing contact, until the near-side foreleg can also be placed in the correct position, should this be necessary. Whether it is or not, it is wise to touch the leg and pretend to put it in position even if it is in the same place, so that the puppy gets the idea of being touched and his legs being moved about. Then, slowly but firmly, slide the hand across the top of the back until it reaches the hindquarters. Then firmly place the rear legs in the positions desired. Again, as with the forelegs, move them about so that the dog becomes accustomed to this procedure.

As soon as the dog is in the correct position let him know that he has done well and pat him and talk to him while he remains in this pose. At first he is bound to wonder whatever strange antic his handler has thought of now, and he will more than likely try and take a flying leap off the table. But again he can be soothed and talked to quietly, and while he is still small he can be picked up bodily and placed in the correct position as previously. Dobermanns have such a proud bearing that to train them for a show stance is extraordinarily easy.

As soon as the puppy has learnt the stance and what is expected of him and how long he has to remain still, then get a member of the family to go over him as a judge would, opening his mouth, etc. The lessons must always be short and, as he becomes more accustomed to this handling, get a stranger who is good with dogs to pretend that he is a judge. A little early, careful training will pay remarkable dividends for years to come in the show ring. Eventually the whole procedure can be repeated on the ground as in a normal show.

There is one other point which is perhaps worth mentioning, and that is the Dobermann's movement. All dogs will move more easily at one speed than at any other, so that it is important for the handler to find out which speed shows up his dog to the greatest advantage. As he is moving the dog himself, this is difficult to ascertain, and so it is better to get a knowledgeable person to watch the handler move the dog at various speeds, and when the correct one becomes obvious the handler must remember that this particular speed is for this particular dog. It is strange indeed how such small points may make the difference between winning and losing. The temperament of both the handler and the Dobermann can be equally affected. A nervous handler will pass this on to his all-too-intelligent Dobermann who will react accordingly; whereas a confident handler, who knows his dog should win, will transmit this feeling to his dog, and win they will.

THE BOISTEROUS STAGE

Dobermann puppies go through a boisterous stage during which they can cause great pain if they happen to treat an ankle or a wrist as if it were a juicy bone. Give him his own toy and never slap the puppy when he is playing. Wear trousers and boots and thick gloves, so that his sharp, strong little teeth will cause less painful damage. The boisterous stage luckily does not last long. When bringing a puppy into a new home which has an older family dog, care must be taken to introduce them to each other carefully and slowly. The old dog is bound to feel a little jealous and resentful of the bouncing newcomer, and unless extreme tact and care are used the newcomer could be seriously injured or frightened.

CHAPTER 4

BREEDING AND THE VALUE OF THE PEDIGREE

BEFORE EMBARKING on the breeding of dogs it is as well to realize that few indeed are the breeders who make money solely out of the dogs themselves, and this is particularly so with Dobermanns. The breeders who do make money generally run boarding kennels, pet shops or poodle parlours or some such business, so that the losses on Dobermann breeding are balanced out by the other businesses. The small breeder, of course, who does not have to advertise and who goes to few shows may well make a little pin-money from a couple of litters.

It is wise to remember that it is just as expensive to rear a litter of poor-quality puppies as it is to rear a superb litter. The breeder will encounter the same complications in whelping, the same inoculation bills, the same cost of registering the puppies, and the enormous cost of rearing Dobermann puppies. But what he loses is the satisfaction of breeding worthwhile stock and seeing each generation of Dobermanns growing up as an improvement upon the previous generation. Even the most skilful breeder will always have some puppies which do not come up to expectation, however carefully the breeding has been planned. The key to good breeding is the elimination of *all* stock not up to standard, and to cull all weakling puppies.

It is better to save up for one good stud fee, and to have only one litter every three years, than to breed a bitch to a bad stud dog twice during the same period. Unfortunately, there are many breeders who are incapable of recognizing a good, sound bitch or stud dog. Some honestly cannot see the good and bad points, and others suffer from an extraordinary disease in the dog world known as 'kennel blindness'. This means that they can see no faults in their own stock but only in the stock of other breeders, of whom subconsciously they are jealous, and they will go to immense pains to criticize the dogs of their rivals.

61

There are certain terms used in breeding that all breeders should know and understand. What, for instance, is 'in-breeding', 'line-breeding' and 'out-crossing'? There has been much discussion in the press and on television about the dangers of in-breeding—so much so that the general public hold up their hands in horror at the idea of deliberate in-breeding. This shows an entire lack of knowledge of its implications, as some of the best cattle, horses and dogs have been produced by constantly repeated in-breeding. But the operative word here is that *all* the animals which have been mated together have been absolutely *sound*, and that *all* animals which were not up to standard have been ruthlessly eliminated. Unless this is done, there is nothing so detrimental to a breed as to mate together two closely related, unsound animals. The breeder who resorts to this type of ignorant breeding is heading for a downfall and rapid deterioration of his stock.

The only difference between 'in-breeding' and 'line-breeding' is in degree, as both involve the breeding together of relatives. In-breeding is the mating together of close relatives, such as parent to son or daughter, brother to sister, uncle and aunt to nephew or niece; whereas mating farther away in relationship is known as 'line-breeding'. This may be so distant that perhaps there is only one name in the pedigree which occurs in both the sire's pedigree and also that of the dam. The more distant the relationship, the more varied in type are the offspring likely to be.

The clever, wise and knowledgeable breeder will in-breed when necessary, he will closely line-breed frequently, and he will resort to an out-cross—that is, mating to an unrelated dog —when he wishes to incorporate some particular feature or to correct a fault in his line or strain. When an out-cross is resorted to, at least two bitches should be mated to the out-cross and their offspring again mated to the same out-cross, or to a near relative with the strong points which are required. The offspring of this second generation should then be line-bred or even in-bred back to the original line or strain, depending on its soundness. Good matings are grandparents to grandchildren and half-brothers to half-sisters. In-breeding in all animals tends to produce rather highly-strung offspring, which are often bad doers and are a worry to their owners. The classic example of this is to be seen in the thoroughbred racehorse as compared, say, with the average hunter.

The result of an out-cross can often be disappointing, because new faults may be added to the strain which had previously been eliminated, and therefore extensive knowledge of the out-cross stock is essential. Many breeders mate their bitches to the reigning champions of the day, using a different line or strain each time. This sort of haphazard breeding will never produce good stock, unless the champions are connected with each other. Often, a breeder will try one champion and find that the resulting puppies, which were entirely an out-cross, are most disappointing, and he will tell all and sundry that that particular champion is no good as a sire; but he should persevere and mate the best bitch of the litter back to the champion or to a near relation of the champion, and with the resulting stock he should again go back, so that there is line-breeding for at least three generations.

Starting a kennel strain can be fascinating, if stock from one well-known kennel are mated cleverly with stock of the correct type of another kennel. The resultant offspring must be line-bred backwards and forwards to each other, eliminating the dogs which are not up to standard and breeding only from the best and most typical.

Faults in a line can just as easily be bred out as required characteristics can be bred into a line. Therefore, before mating a bitch study her pedigree, be sure that she is sound, and ask a knowledgeable breeder what stud dog he recommends that she be mated to. If that tallies with what is written above, and you have seen the prospective stud dog and scrutinized his pedigree, and approved of both, go ahead with your breeding programme.

A large kennel, breeding seriously, should have at least three lines going at the same time. It is best if they are all connected slightly, so that when the breeder resorts to out-crossing it is not likely to produce very varied stock. It must be remembered that in-breeding or line-breeding can only produce what is already in the stock. Nothing new can be added, although some features are hidden and will only become apparent with experimenting.

Genetics are too complicated a subject for a book such as this. But the breeder will hear such terms as 'double-dominant genes', 'double-recessive genes' and 'dominant-recessive genes'. Each pair of genes is inherited, one from each parent. The most important genes to be aware of are the dominant-recessive genes, as the recessive characteristics can appear in future generations.

It is worth remembering that ten pairs of genes go to make up the coat, and this explains the coat variations in the breed. Blues, for instance, have the least density of coat, followed by the fawns and then the browns. As an example of the power of the recessive gene, light eyes and light nose are recessive, and dogs mated together with these light colours will always produce offspring of the same light colours ('double-recessive'). Whereas, when black-nosed and dark-eyed dogs are mated together, if there is a light-nosed ancestor in both backgrounds ('dominant-recessive') these matings can produce light-nosed puppies. Thus, when planning a mating, it is always important to bear in mind the hidden recessive genes.

Another useful principle to remember is that a gene pair is only of one strength. By this I mean that a dog with a certain recessive characteristic that has been bred from two dogs with equivalent dominant-recessive characteristics has nevertheless received a recessive gene pair; and that if he is mated to a similarly bred bitch he should sire progeny with just as good examples of the recessive characteristics as a dog with a pedigree showing this characteristic for several generations back.

Unfortunately, not all genes are either wholly dominant or wholly recessive. Some are more dominant than others and vice versa. As a result, although matings tend to produce the results indicated, they will not always produce certain gene pairs in the exact averages expected, and sometimes the recessive gene will show itself to a lesser or greater extent in combination with the dominant gene.

Two dogs with the same fault should never be mated together. It is, moreover, useless to mate a dog with short legs to a bitch with very long legs, hoping to get all the puppies with medium-sized legs. Some of the puppies will take after the long-legged parent, whilst the others will be short-legged. However, mate the best of the puppies back to a dog of the same line with the legs of the size that are being aimed at, repeat this in the next two generations, and eventually the length of leg required will be obtained. (Long legs are recessive.)

There is no doubt that there are some stud dogs and bitches with very dominant characteristics, and, regardless of whom they are mated to, they will always produce puppies with their own characteristics. There are also some matings which are out-crosses, where the stud dog and bitch just seem to click and produce outstanding puppies which may go on to become famous champions; but, because they are out-crosses, they themselves are extremely unlikely to produce outstanding puppies.

This perhaps is enough to show that breeding requires knowledge, time and money, in order to experiment. The real enjoyment in breeding is the constant striving for perfection. No breeder should ever be satisfied with the mediocre puppies which may make money but which can give no real satisfaction, pleasure or sense of achievement.

A 'strain' is a term used for a family of dogs which are closely related, all of whom strongly resemble each other. These dogs, wherever they appear, are always easily recognizable, owing to the strong strain of their breeding.

BREEDING FOR ERECT EARS

If erect ears are desired in the breed, then breeders must think carefully how this can be done without spoiling the rest of the breeding of the Dobermann. It would be exceedingly difficult to produce erect ears without recourse to some other breed, and this would horrify a great many people.

Very occasionally, Dobermanns have been born with naturally erect ears and one such bitch was apparently mated back to her sire in order to try to fix this characteristic. Unfortunately, the experiment failed, and the chances were that it would. If the bitch had been mated back to her sire a number of times or to her brothers with the smallest and most erect ears, the chances would have been quite good of reproducing the erect ears. Breeders are apt to give up too quickly when success does not come with the first mating.

In order to try to establish erect ears in the Dobermann, an experiment might be made in which three 8 lb. English Toy Terrier (black-and-tan) dogs with excellent ear qualities for many generations would be mated to three of the largest, most typical, Dobermann bitches with small ears. The largest dog of one of the resultant litters having the smallest erect ears should be mated to a bitch of one of the other litters with the smallest erect ears looking most like a Dobermann. By selective breeding, using only the largest stock with the smallest pricked ears for each mating and culling all stock which were too small or which had soft and large ears, erect ears would become fixed since they are the dominant gene. It would probably take three or four generations of careful, selective breeding. Unfortunately, with the existing Kennel Club ruling, it would take longer to get a Class One Registration, because the dog with the correct ears would finally have to be mated to a pure Dobermann with soft ears, and the offspring would at first only count as 'crossbred'; and similar matings would have to continue until the pricked-eared dog had four generations of its pedigree with one parent being a Class One classified Dobermann.

If there were a really strong-charactered breeder who really wished to produce Dobermanns with erect ears, the Kennel Club might be persuaded to make a special dispensation, if the other breed used was the English Toy Terrier, because indirectly through the Manchester Terrier this was part of the breeding of the original Dobermann. The breeder who could organize this might perhaps be permitted to give his name towards the resultant natural prick-eared Dobermanns, and they could for example be called 'Smith Dobermanns'.

It would certainly be an extremely interesting experiment for someone to undertake, and there would be no need for breeders to hold up their hands in horror since, after all, all breeds are man-made.

The disparity in size between the two breeds would not be insurmountable, as I have known a Boxer bitch mate a Dachshund without any human assistance.

As an example of how easily and, indeed, how quickly erect

ears could be introduced into the Dobermann, the Bull Terrier used to have dropped ears, but selective breeding has produced fine, erect ears in that breed. This was done in four or five generations, and it could be accomplished in the Dobermann with comparable ease and speed. The main problem is the choice of the most suitable breed to use as the out-cross, and its solution would be facilitated by the complete co-operation of all Dobermann breeders.

THE PEDIGREE

Although a pedigree is just a tabulated list of names with the champions often written in red, it can reveal a great deal of information. On the other hand, it can be completely meaningless. The best pedigrees to read are those which are made out with as much information as possible. Each dog should have its Kennel Club registration number entered underneath.

The pedigree should contain the colour, height, weight, temperament and working ability of each dog, and perhaps a set of symbols regarding the genetic make-up; for example, the head, eyes, ears, mouth, etc. If these are good, they are allotted capital letters; if bad, small letters; and if good but the background is known not to be particularly good, a capital letter with a little letter beside it. Of course, if photographs can be supplied for each dog in the pedigree, then the pedigree becomes intensely useful and helpful, and obviously far more interesting, especially to the serious breeder. Owners of stud dogs would be well advised to keep a pedigree such as this. It takes a little trouble to do, but it is extremely rewarding.

COLOUR BREEDING

Colour breeding is particularly important in the Dobermann. The colour and markings have been selectively bred for over a period of a great many years. As a result the bright rust-red markings are sharply defined and appear above each eye, and on the muzzle, the throat and the fore-chest, on all legs and feet, and also below the tail. White markings of any kind are heavily penalized in the show ring. In the U.S.A. white markings on the chest must not exceed one-half a square inch. The problem in colour breeding for the Dobermann is to keep the clear rust-red marking bright. Care must be taken with the black dogs, because if the pigmentation becomes too dark it covers the rich tan, which consequently becomes dull. This is known as melanism, which, if it is allowed to continue, gradually erases the tan markings, so that they become indistinct and could eventually disappear altogether. It is this beautiful marking on the face of a Dobermann which gives it its distinguished and expressive head. The best method to keep the tan markings really rich is occasionally to mate the pure black-and-tan dogs to the browns, or to a black dog with a brown parent (a hybrid). This tends to enhance and maintain the rich colour marking. Pure black-and-tan is the easiest colour to breed and so far in England the tan markings have not deteriorated in richness, and an out-cross to improve the colour has not yet been necessary.

There are a great many varied shades of brown in the breed. Blues are really a form of black, although some blues come from the same recessive gene which creates the browns, and browns and blacks mated together often produce blues. The coat markings also pair with the pigmentation of the skin, so that, generally speaking, the darker the coat the darker are the eyes and the pigmentation of the skin in general. The latter includes the rims of the eyes, the lips, the interior lining of the ears, and the nose. The browns are due to a recessive gene, and it is these which require the most thought when breeding. Once the light-coloured recessive genes are brought into a breed they will always reappear when two dogs each carrying them are mated together. Their offspring will normally never again produce the dark pigmentation unless and until they are mated back to dogs of the dominant dark colour. If two browns are mated together only brown puppies will be produced owing to the resultant double-recessive gene pair. Two blues mated together will produce black, blue and brown puppies in the proportion of 1:2:1, owing to the effect of the dominant-recessive gene pairs. Pure black-and-tans mated to pure black-and-tans can produce only black-and-tan offspring as this is a dominant gene. These dogs all have the black pigmentation of the inside of the ear.

Blues and browns mated to each other should produce equal

numbers of blues and browns, but no blacks. Blacks and blues mated to each other will normally produce equal numbers of blues and blacks, but no browns. Blues and browns are considered to be better colours for the tropics, but black-and-tans are easier to breed as their eyes and pigmentation will never be a problem, unless the recessive gene for light colour is in their ancestry.

The 'Isabella' colour is an indeterminate fawn, which is not recognized. It is a Spanish word by origin. Queen Isabella of Spain refused to change her blouse doubtlet until the siege of Granada was over. To the present day the expression is used for a child with a dirty front, and also for a wild bird which has a dirty fawn breast.

The colour of young puppies changes, but the blacker and darker the puppy is at birth the clearer and brighter will be the tan marking when it is adult. Black puppies born with a brown tinge to their coat have a dominant recessive gene pair for colour, and may transmit either a dominant or a recessive gene to their offspring. Some puppies are born with white feet, but these disappear as they grow older. Blue puppies are a real mouse-grey at birth, but their colour will change.

One of the difficulties in the breeding of Dobermanns is getting rid of any white marking on the chest; and judges and breeders will discard these dogs, regardless of how perfect they may be in all other qualities, such as in soundness, typical conformation, superb temperament and working ability. This sort of breed fetish is one of the greatest tragedies in dog breeding, and it is the cause of the incidence of many unsound dogs in many breeds. In the U.S.A. more than half a square inch of white on a Dobermann results in the automatic disqualification of an otherwise perfect dog, whilst an unsound but correctly marked dog could go forward to become a champion. Breeders in all breeds require to bring breeding priorities into perspective. Soundness should always take precedence over a patch of white or a light eye or some such minor show defect.

CHAPTER 5

THE BROOD BITCH AND WHELPING

THE CHOICE of the brood bitch for the foundation of a kennel is of the utmost importance. As the old adage goes: 'A kennel is as good as its bitches.' First and foremost, the bitch must be a typical specimen, she must be sound and have an excellent temperament. She should be free from shyness, nervousness and any form of viciousness. Dobermanns generally whelp easily; nevertheless the bitch should come from a self-whelping line or strain. A brood bitch should have no outstanding faults, particularly bad hereditary ones, such as a bad temperament. A bitch should also come from good working stock. If a bitch of this calibre is found, study her pedigree, find out all you can about her ancestors, their size, and whether they are free from the common hereditary defects; note if the breeding is good—that is to say, whether there is some line-breeding on both sides of the pedigree, and avoid a bitch which is too in-bred.

The perfect dog, of course, does not exist, so it is usually better to choose a bitch with perhaps only one fault rather than a mediocre bitch with no outstanding qualities; but, whatever bitch is finally chosen, good temperament is perhaps the most important of all traits. It is certainly easier to breed out one fault than to breed in a number of typical points which are lacking in a particular bitch. Choose a bitch from a reputable breeder, where you can see the ancestors and can put your trust in the breeder, particularly if you are a novice.

Ask the breeder to advise you on the best choice of a sire for the new bitch. Naturally, all breeders will suggest that you use one of their own stud dogs, which is perfectly correct information as far as line-breeding is concerned. But it is just possible that the novice breeder would like to start a line of his own by using a stud dog from another well-known kennel, which would probably be a complete out-cross. Provided that the breeding is good the dogs typical, it is quite a good idea to work out your own breeding programme, making your own line and eventually your own strain. But this will take many years of trial and error, and, having started, it is imperative to continue for at least four generations of good line-breeding before your results can be expected to pay off. If, however, after this time your stock is not up to the standard you had hoped, cut your losses, part with all your stock, and start again. It is a waste of time and energy and quite pointless to breed only pet dogs. It is also detrimental to a breed, for there will always be some people who will breed from these pet dogs; instead of the breed improving all the time, it can quickly deteriorate, both physically and temperamentally, and become unpopular, and then even the pet puppies cannot be sold easily.

Choose a bitch between the age of four and ten months, and if you can afford to buy two from the same line, so much the better. The older the bitch, naturally, the more you will have to pay for a good one, but you will know exactly what you are buying. A novice might be wise to buy a bitch who has already whelped and reared a litter. This will be even more expensive, because, if the bitch is really good, few breeders are willing to part with such a gem.

It must be remembered that the bitch will pass on half her genetic qualities to her puppies, so that the strength of any kennel, as I have mentioned previously, lies in the quality of its bitches. The bitch will be yours for all her life, whilst you can choose a different stud dog at each mating.

Having acquired the best bitch that you can afford, allow her to settle down in her new environment before mating her to the stud dog of your choice. A Dobermann bitch may be mated, provided that she is sound enough and mature enough and mentally suitable, after the age of one year. She should never ideally be mated before this, as she will not be fully developed to cope with a large litter, which Dobermanns so frequently have.

All bitches, if they are to be bred from, should be mated before the age of five years. If they are mated for the first time after this age, there may possibly be whelping complications. A good rule, therefore, is not to mate a Dobermann for the first time before the age of one year, nor after the age of five years. It is probably better that a bitch should not be mated more frequently than alternate seasons—that is, that she should have only one litter a year. But if a bitch has small litters of under six puppies, then she could be mated two seasons running and rested at her next season. If, however, the bitch has the normal large Dobermann litters of nine to fifteen puppies, then she should only be mated once a year. There is no hard-and-fast rule about the mating of a bitch, but to use her as a puppy machine is inhuman and mating a bitch too frequently is bound to have a deleterious effect on the whelps. The second litter is frequently the best litter of all, and therefore it would be wise to go out to the best possible stud for this mating. A stud dog usually begets his best offspring at the age of about three and three-quarter years. A bitch should not really be expected to have any more litters after the age of seven years.

Before embarking on the mating of a Dobermann it is as well to find out if there is any likelihood of having difficulty in finding homes for the puppies. Very often the breeder of the bitch or the owner of the stud dog will help in this matter, and it is then usual, for this assistance, to offer 10% of the sale price. If the litter is a good one, the breeder of the bitch might buy in the best of the litter, or even the entire litter, and this is a very good idea from the point of view of the novice, especially as the cost of rearing Dobermann puppies well is extremely expensive and very hard work.

THE SEASON

A bitch generally first comes into season at the age of seven months, although some may come in a little earlier and others later. The season may go unnoticed for the first few days, if the bitches keep themselves clean and the swelling of the vulva is not detected. The first sign is usually the frequency of urination. The season generally lasts about three weeks but can last longer, and during this time it is essential that the bitch should be kept securely shut up away from all dogs. If a bitch is not to be mated, never allow her to have a hormone injection to prevent her season. Once the hormone cycle is disturbed it may never come right again.

The best days to mate a bitch are probably the eleventh and thirteenth days. Some breeders prefer the tenth and twelfth days. There is, however, no hard-and-fast rule, as each bitch may differ from others, and individual bitches can differ from season to season. I have known a bitch to be ready for mating as early as the fifth day, and another one was mated successfully on the twenty-eighth day. The bitch's urine during her season is exciting to dogs, and she should be prevented from urinating where she will attract them.

The season is usually first noticed when the vulva starts to harden and swell. This is followed by a show of bright red blood, which in turn gradually becomes paler as the vulva softens. The bitch becomes interested in other bitches if there are any and will play with them and twist her tail. This is a sign that she is nearly ready for her mating. Test her for colour; but this is not always an infallible test and only a guide. Place a clean piece of cotton-wool or white absorbent toilet paper on the vulva, and if the discharge is a pale pink arrange to have her mated immediately.

There is a glucose fertility test which is easy to do to ascertain the correct day for mating. This is useful particularly if the stud dog lives a considerable distance away. Tes-tape, as it is called, can be bought from a chemist, and is the same tape as is used for human diabetes. At the beginning of the season there is no glucose secreted in the vagina; this builds up slowly and when the glucose secretion is at its maximum a piece of Tes-tape inserted into the vagina will be turned bright green after a few seconds. The bitch will be ready to mate twenty-four hours later.

As soon as a bitch comes into season, or preferably just before, she should be wormed. The owner of the stud dog to be used must be informed as early as possible, so that a date for the mating about ten days later can be definitely booked.

A bitch should only be mated when she is in perfect health; she should not be overweight or too thin. She should be free from internal and external parasites, although it is possible to worm a bitch within three weeks of mating without harming the puppies.

PREGNANCY

The signs of pregnancy vary from bitch to bitch, and some can conceal their secret surprisingly well, especially if there is only a small litter. On the other hand, Dobermanns are well known for their large litters, and so pregnancy may often become apparent as early as the third week; but with a small litter of two or three it may not be noticed until the bitch is sleeping and abdominal movements are observed as late as only ten days before the bitch is due to whelp. During pregnancy the bitch should lead a normal life with a regular amount of exercise; and extra nourishing food, especially additional protein, calcium and egg yolk, should be added to the diet daily from the fourth or fifth week. Give the bitch as much meat as she will eat, unless she is very greedy. Her daily ration of meat should be increased by one-quarter, gradually building up to double the quantity by the seventh week. It is best to give the bitch two meals a day. If the bitch is overweight her normal rations should be cut down accordingly. Stress can be added to one meal a day, and, of course, the usual drops of capsules of vitamins should be continued. During the last four weeks the bitch should be given daily a quarter of a teaspoonful of coloidal calcium with vitamin D. This provides extra calcium required by the bitch, and also makes whelping easier and helps to prevent eclampsia. On no account should more than this dosage be given.

GESTATION PERIOD

The normal gestation period is sixty-three days, but the majority of Dobermanns have their puppies two or three days early.

Puppies can survive if whelped as early as the fifty-seventh day and as late as the seventy-first day, but if a bitch has not had her puppies by the sixty-third day, taking into account the day of a second mating, always inform the vet. Let the vet know, about a week beforehand, the approximate day that the bitch is due to whelp, in case his services should be required, but most bitches manage everything easily themselves.

ATTENDING THE WHELPING BITCH

If it is the first time that you have attended a bitch whelping, make certain that a discreet eye is kept on her from time to time,

GESTATION TABLE
Showing when your bitch is due to whelp.

MATED JANUARY	DUE TO WHELP MARCH	MATED FEBRUARY	DUE TO WHELP APRIL	MATED MARCH	DUE TO WHELP MAY	MATED APRIL	DUE TO WHELP JUNE	MATED MAY	DUE TO WHELP JULY	MATED JUNE	DUE TO WHELP AUGUST	MATED JULY	DUE TO WHELP SEPTEMBER	MATED AUGUST	DUE TO WHELP OCTOBER	MATED SEPTEMBER	DUE TO WHELP NOVEMBER	MATED OCTOBER	DUE TO WHELP DECEMBER	MATED NOVEMBER	DUE TO WHELP JANUARY	MATED DECEMBER	DUE TO WHELP FEBRUARY
1	5	1	5	1	3	1	3	1	3	1	3	1	2	1	3	1	3	1	3	1	3	1	2
2	6	2	6	2	4	2	4	2	4	2	4	2	3	2	4	2	4	2	4	2	4	2	3
3	7	3	7	3	5	3	5	3	5	3	5	3	4	3	5	3	5	3	5	3	5	3	4
4	8	4	8	4	6	4	6	4	6	4	6	4	5	4	6	4	6	4	6	4	6	4	5
5	9	5	9	5	7	5	7	5	7	5	7	5	6	5	7	5	7	5	7	5	7	5	6
6	10	6	10	6	8	6	8	6	8	6	8	6	7	6	8	6	8	6	8	6	8	6	7
7	11	7	11	7	9	7	9	7	9	7	9	7	8	7	9	7	9	7	9	7	9	7	8
8	12	8	12	8	10	8	10	8	10	8	10	8	9	8	10	8	10	8	10	8	10	8	9
9	13	9	13	9	11	9	11	9	11	9	11	9	10	9	11	9	11	9	11	9	11	9	10
10	14	10	14	10	12	10	12	10	12	10	12	10	11	10	12	10	12	10	12	10	12	10	11
11	15	11	15	11	13	11	13	11	13	11	13	11	12	11	13	11	13	11	13	11	13	11	12
12	16	12	16	12	14	12	14	12	14	12	14	12	13	12	14	12	14	12	14	12	14	12	13
13	17	13	17	13	15	13	15	13	15	13	15	13	14	13	15	13	15	13	15	13	15	13	14
14	18	14	18	14	16	14	16	14	16	14	16	14	15	14	16	14	16	14	16	14	16	14	15
15	19	15	19	15	17	15	17	15	17	15	17	15	16	15	17	15	17	15	17	15	17	15	16
16	20	16	20	16	18	16	18	16	18	16	18	16	17	16	18	16	18	16	18	16	18	16	17
17	21	17	21	17	19	17	19	17	19	17	19	17	18	17	19	17	19	17	19	17	19	17	18
18	22	18	22	18	20	18	20	18	20	18	20	18	19	18	20	18	20	18	20	18	20	18	19
19	23	19	23	19	21	19	21	19	21	19	21	19	20	19	21	19	21	19	21	19	21	19	20
20	24	20	24	20	22	20	22	20	22	20	22	20	21	20	22	20	22	20	22	20	22	20	21
21	25	21	25	21	23	21	23	21	23	21	23	21	22	21	23	21	23	21	23	21	23	21	22
22	26	22	26	22	24	22	24	22	24	22	24	22	23	22	24	22	24	22	24	22	24	22	23
23	27	23	27	23	25	23	25	23	25	23	25	23	24	23	25	23	25	23	25	23	25	23	24
24	28	24	28	24	26	24	26	24	26	24	26	24	25	24	26	24	26	24	26	24	26	24	25
25	29	25	29	25	27	25	27	25	27	25	27	25	26	25	27	25	27	25	27	25	27	25	26
26	30	26	30	26	28	26	28	26	28	26	28	26	27	26	28	26	28	26	28	26	28	26	27
27	31	27	May 1	27	29	27	29	27	29	27	29	27	28	27	29	27	29	27	29	27	29	27	28
28	Apl 1	28	2	28	30	28	30	28	30	28	30	28	29	28	30	28	30	28	30	28	30	28	Mar 1
29	2	29	3	29	31	29	July 1	29	31	29	31	29	30	29	31	29	Dec 1	29	31	29	31	29	2
30	3	—	—	30	June 1	30	2	30	Aug 1	30	Sept 1	30	Oct 1	30	Nov 1	30	2	30	Jan 1	30	Feb 1	30	3
31	4	—	—	31	2	—	—	31	2	—	—	31	2	31	2	—	—	31	2	—	—	31	4

just in case there are any complications, which luckily are not common in Dobermanns. Most bitches prefer to whelp by themselves unaided, but no bitch should really be allowed to whelp entirely alone without some form of supervision. Breech presentations are quite normal but may require assistance. Make notes in a notebook of the various stages and of the time of arrival of each whelp. See Dogs and How to Breed Them by John Gifford.

HOW OFTEN TO BREED A BITCH

The wise breeder enters up for each bitch the details about mating, whelping, and when the next season is due. A bitch generally comes into season again between four and eight months after the birth of her puppies. It is best to mate a bitch at alternate seasons, unless she is irregular and the seasons are far apart. A bitch should not be mated if she has recently suffered a serious illness or is out of condition.

Generally, a bitch continues to have puppies up to the age of seven years, but after this she may well feel that she has had enough of such nonsense and cease to have any more puppies. There are a few bitches who will whelp normally and easily up to the age of ten years, but no bitch should be expected to have more than six litters at the outside, and never more than two caesarians. A bitch must never whelp or nurse a litter wearing any form of collar or lead.

WHELPING

THE WHELPING BOX About a week before the bitch is due to whelp, make her used to her special whelping box, which should be 3 feet by 4 feet and 1½ feet high, and 6 inches off the ground. It should be provided with a whelping bar across one end, or, better still, on all four sides, to prevent her lying on a puppy during the birth of another one. A special room, a garage, or a shed are all perfectly good places for her to whelp, provided that they are dry and draught-proof. Line the bottom of the box with a piece of vinyl and cover it with layers of thick newspaper, which can be easily disposed of. Give the bitch her blanket or a sheet until the actual birth of the whelps. The bitch must be under observation for the entire week before she is due to whelp, in case she should do so early.

INFRA-RED LAMP. The breeder should own an infra-red lamp, which can be suspended from the ceiling about 3 feet above the whelping box to keep the puppies warm. This is especially necessary just after their birth. Gradually, the lamp can be raised as the puppies become older and require less heat. The only way to know whether the heat is being maintained is by the use of a thermometer in the box. This should register 70°F. (21°C.) for the first week, and then the temperature can be gradually reduced to 60°F. (15.6°C.). There should be a bowl of water constantly near the box, to counteract the dryness of the air caused by the infra-red lamp.

WHELPING TRAY. In case a bitch should require any assistance, it is as well to set a tray with some articles which might be required. These should include some cotton-wool, Dettol, artery forceps, a handkerchief or piece of cotton material, some brandy, an eye-dropper, a jar of Vaseline, warm olive oil, a small rough towel for drying the whelps, scales for weighing them, a clock for timing the whelping and the time between births, a notebook for writing up the details for future reference, and the telephone number of the nearest vet.

START OF LABOUR. Twenty-four hours before whelping the temperature of the bitch will drop to 99°F. (37.2°C.), the normal temperature being 101.2°F. (38.4°C.). The vagina softens and there is a sticky discharge. Labour is divided into three stages. In the first stage the bitch becomes restless and licks her rear parts. She may pass urine frequently, and she will start to tear up the newspaper and make a nest just before the arrival of the first whelp. The bitch generally refuses all food and is occasionally sick. This uncomfortable stage may last as long as twenty-four hours, but more frequently it is a matter of a few hours only.

The second stage is when the pains change to powerful contractions, which can be seen and felt by placing the hand upon the abdomen, where the hardening of the uterus can be felt easily. These pains last a few seconds and then the bitch rests in between. The pains continue until the whelp is born. The first sign of the whelp's impending arrival will be a hardening beneath the bitch's tail. The bitch should never be permitted to push in the second stage for more than two hours without getting help from the vet.

The membrane or water-bag usually makes the first appearance and contains a greenish fluid which protects the whelp before it is born and dilates the vaginal passage. Inside this is the whelp, which is covered in another membrane. The water-bag looks like a dark slimy skin and it may appear and disappear again with each contraction. The bag varies in size according to the length of time before it breaks. Sometimes the bag breaks early, in which case it may not be noticed, but the vet should be informed if no whelp has arrived within two hours after the bag is known to have burst, and if there is no sign of labour.

The third stage of labour is the expulsion of the placenta.

ARRIVAL OF THE WHELPS. The whelps generally arrive at intervals of between ten and thirty minutes, either head first or hind feet first. If there is a delay of an hour in the birth of a whelp, veterinary assistance should be sought. Keep an eye on the bitch, especially when she is biting the cords. She may have difficulty and bite them off to close to the puppy, which is dangerous, and sometimes causes a haemorrhage, a hernia or an infection later. If the bitch is slow in breaking the membrane from the puppy, break it by the puppy's nose so that it can start breathing. If the puppy is not breathing normally, hold it upside down and give it a small shake to dislodge any fluid which may have got into the air passages. The bitch noses her puppies about quite roughly, which gets them breathing, and she licks them and dries them. The puppies are very quick in finding the milk bar, but if one is slow or weak it should be put on to a teat. After the birth of each puppy the placenta, or after-birth, comes away and most bitches eat this, although probably two or three are sufficient. If more are eaten they are inclined to cause the bitch diarrhoea. Care should be taken to see that a puppy does not get behind the bitch when she is having the next whelp as she can easily accidentally squash it. If some bitches are particularly rough and the puppies are arriving quickly, it is a good idea to remove them and dry them for her on a rough towel and to keep them under an infrared lamp until all are born safely. Taking the puppies away may worry the bitch; if this is so, allow her to keep a few. She may not miss the others while she is busy cleaning the puppies and eating the placentas. As soon as the last puppy has been born, return all of them to the dam, putting them on teats.

If there is a puppy having difficulty in breathing, weak smelling-salts are excellent and artificial respiration can be given. (See Chapter 10—'Ailments and Useful Hints'.) The bitch can be offered a little warm milk and glucose while she is resting between the births of successive whelps, but she will often refuse this. If the whelping is long, take the bitch out to relieve herself from time to time.

Unless you are sure that all the placentas are out, it is probably wise to get the vet to examine the bitch to make certain that all is well with her and that there is not a retained whelp. Also if any puppies are to be culled, then this is the moment to do it.

BREECH PRESENTATION. If the whelp is coming hind feet first, it is imperative to get it out quickly. Take hold of the feet with some cotton-wool or a handkerchief to prevent them from slipping, and draw the whelp round between the bitch's legs and towards her nose. It is essential to get the puppy out quickly, as its blood supply will have been cut off and it will have no oxygen. The whelps can stand quite a strong pull without any damage occurring.

TO BREAK THE CORD. Except in certain circumstances it is always better to tear the cord rather than to cut it, as this prevents any haemorrhage and obviates the necessity of tying the cord. It is important to pull the cord towards the puppy when breaking it, in order to prevent an umbilical hernia. Artery forceps are extremely useful for clamping the cord, as a good grip is obtained and the placenta can then be drawn out easily.

EXAMINATION. As soon as all the puppies are born, place clean paper in the box. It is advisable to examine each puppy for a cleft palate or any other deformity. Offer the bitch a little warm milk and glucose, and then leave her to rest quietly for several hours. After a long rest take the bitch out for quick run to relieve herself.

Occasionally, some puppies are weak and slow to start feeding. In this case, open the puppy's mouth with a teat by pressing the teat on to the bottom jaw. As soon as the puppy opens its mouth, insert the teat and hold the puppy on to it until it has achieved a good suction. It should then be able to stay on the teat by itself, but keep watching every few hours to make sure that all the puppies are feeding.

COLOSTRUM. The bitch provides colostrum in her teats for the first few days. This fluid is very important to the puppies as it is rich in antibodies, which give the puppies protection in their first months. The milk comes in gradually about the fourth day and the colostrum then gradually becomes weaker.

Immediately after the birth of the puppies the bitch has a discharge which is bloodstained and often changes to a dark greeny colour on coming into contact with the air. The bitch's temperature usually remains at about 103°F. (39.4°C.) for forty-eight hours, but it should return to normal on the third day. If the temperature remains up, or if there is a bad smell from a discharge, inform the vet immediately. There may be a retained whelp or placenta. If the bitch should suffer any diarrhoea give her a little kaolin mixture for three days.

Occasionally, a novice notices that a bitch is straining and mistakes this for constipation. If it happens before the arrival of the puppies, then she is in labour and is probably just about to produce one. If straining continues after the birth of all the puppies, there may be a tear at the cervix of the uterus. If it should occur a day after the arrival of the puppies, it could be another whelp, but it is more likely to be a retained placenta. Take the bitch's temperature, and if it is up get her to a vet immediately. The bitch by this time is probably dangerously ill.

AFTER-CARE OF THE BITCH

After the birth of all the litter give the bitch a little glucose and milk, or even a little Farex. Leave her quietly alone for several hours, then take her out to relieve herself. Refrain from showing off this lovely litter that you are so proud of, until they have their eyes open. Never allow another breeder to touch the puppies for fear of an infection. Both the puppies and the dam require constant observation every three or four hours in the first few days, and they should be kept scrupulously clean. Always make sure that all the puppies are feeding properly, and that the tiny ones are not being pushed off by their larger brothers and sisters. Weak puppies should be put on to the rear teats. If there is a runt in the litter, get the vet to destroy it. These weaklings can cause infections to build up, and may lead to fading puppies. Keep the teats under observation, to see that they do not become hard and hot. If they do, get veterinary assistance.

After the first few days the bitch can be put back on to her normal diet, with egg yolk and plenty of protein and red meat, milk and added vitamins. While the bitch is feeding her puppies she requires a constant supply of fresh, clean water. The puppies should be weighed daily for the first three days and then every other day, and finally once a week. This is an easy but useful thing to do, because if one of the puppies is not thriving it is noticed at once. Infection of a puppy's navel is not uncommon, owing to the bitch biting the cord too close. A bitch should not be expected to rear more than nine puppies; the rest should go to foster-mothers or be destroyed. Culling the puppies should be done by the vet.

CARE OF ORPHAN PUPPIES

Occasionally, the breeder has the misfortune to have to hand rear a litter of puppies. This can be exhausting, but at the same time it is very rewarding when successful. There are many methods of feeding small puppies. The novice generally tends to overfeed the poor little things, so that they get distended stomachs, cry, and soon die. Most breeders have their own pet formula with which to feed orphan puppies, and there are also ready-prepared, dried, puppy milks. But provided that the puppies are a reasonable size, and, more important still, provided that they are strong, then almost any mixture will do the trick. I have known puppies brought up from birth on a Farex and-milk mixture. But if the puppies are small and weak, whatever mixture they are given is often of no avail.

First and foremost, the puppies must be kept really warm at a constant temperature of 95°–100°F. (35°–38°C.) for the first week. The temperature can then be slowly dropped to 75°F. (24°C.) at the age of three weeks. The puppies should be free from draughts and the air should be kept warm by infra-red lamp, with a bowl of water close by to keep the atmosphere moist. It is important that the puppies should never become dehydrated. They require constant observation, as they are very liable to infection, having had no colostrum from the dam to protect them. If it is possible to find a foster mother, so much the better for all concerned, and there is often a kind breeder who can help with one.

FEEDERS. For feeding the puppies a small dropper may be used to begin with, or a small cat's bottle, which costs 75p and can be obtained from Cat's Accessories Limited, 1 Newnham Street, Bedford. The Belcroy bottles are extremely good too. There are also multiple feeding bottles for a number of puppies. But the best of all methods is probably tube feeding.

Set a small tray with all the things necessary for looking after the puppies. This should include:

A dropper, a bottle, or a catheter and a 10-c.c. syringe, depending on the method employed.

A cup containing the formula.

A bottle of Abidec.

A small jar of cotton wool for cleaning the puppies.

A handkerchief for wrapping round each puppy.

A piece of absorbent lavatory paper to use as a bib so that the puppy is kept clean and dry.

A small jar of Nivea cream.

A small rough towel.

FORMULAE. Whatever formula is used, it must be remembered that bitch's milk is very much stronger than cows' milk. The fat and casein content of cows' milk is 3.7% and 3.0% respectively, whilst that of bitch's milk is 10% and 6% respectively.

A very easy formula is a heaped teaspoon of full-cream dried milk added to $2\frac{1}{2}$ oz. of freshly boiled milk. Give three drops of Abidec each day direct into the puppy's mouth.

FEEDING. The number of meals a day should be according to the size and strength of the puppy and also the method used, e.g. dropper, bottle or tube. Feed the puppy according to its weight, not its age. A week old puppy can probably manage on only one night feed. Many can manage without it, but premature puppies require feeding three-hourly throughout the twenty-four hours.

Birling Britta van de Heerhof.
Bred in Holland.
One of the first Dobermanns imported into England. The dam of the first British Champion dog, Champion Wolfox Birling Rogue.
Owner: Mr. L. Hamilton Renwick.

Birling Rachel.
Sire: Birling Bruno von Ehrgarten (Bred in Switzerland and one of the original imports in 1947).
Rachel, a puppy from his only litter in this country before being exported to Hong Kong, was the top winning Dobermann of her day, and was litter sister to Champion Wolfox Birling Rogue.
Owner: Mr. L. Hamilton Renwick.

Puppies sired by Ch. Edencourt's Avenger
Breeder: Mrs. A. E. Hewitt.

Photo: Anne Hewitt.

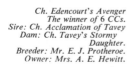

Ch. Edencourt's Avenger
The winner of 6 CCs.
Sire: Ch. Acclamation of Tavey
Dam: Ch. Tavey's Stormy
Daughter.
Breeder: Mr. E. J. Protheroe.
Owner: Mrs. A. E. Hewitt.

Photo: Anne Hewitt.

Ch. Jove of Cartergate.
Sire: Ch. Claus of Cartergate.
Dam: Ch. Helena of Cartergate.
Breeder: Miss E. Would.
Owner: Mrs. O. Morris.

Photo: C. M. Cooke and Son.

Ch. Annastock Lance. The winner of 5 CCs.
Sire: Ch. Tavey's Stormy Achievement.
Breeder/Owner: Mrs. L. J. Parkes.
Photo: Anne Hewitt.

Ch. Triogen Traffic Cop. The winner of 3 CCs. Eleven times Best in Show all Breeds.
Sire: Ch. Acclamation of Tavey.
Breeder/Owner: Mr. A. B. Hogg.
Photo: H. Francis Pilgrim.

Above: *Ch. Clanguard Comanche. The winner of 4 CCs.*
Sire: Ch. Carrickgreen Confederate.
Breeder: Mr. W. Beattie.
Owner: Mrs. H. Morgan.
Photo: William Burke.

Right: *Ch. Cadereyta of Roanoke. The winner of 3 CCs.*
Sire: Ch. Tumlow Impeccable.
Breeder: Mr. J. Hodson.
Owners: Mr. J. and Mrs. D. C. Richardson.
Photo: D. C. Richardson.

Left: *Ch. Triogen Tuppeny Feast. The winner of 6 CCs.*
Sire: Ch. Acclamation of Tavey.
Breeder: Mr. A. B. Hogg.
Owners: Mr. J. and Mrs. D. C. Richardson.
Photo: D. C. Richardson.

until they are well established. It is as well to have a loud alarm clock set every three hours to remind a busy housewife to feed the puppies, as it is usually the poor wife who is landed with the job.

The secret of hand-rearing is not to overfeed. If the puppies sleep from one feed to the next without crying and their stools are formed and contain no undigested curds and they gain weight, then the feeding is correct. The moment curds are seen, which are undigested food and are clearly doing the puppy no good, cut down the mixture but keep the same fluid content. If the puppy seems hungry, slowly increase the food. The first meals must be given slowly, drop by drop, and gradually the puppy will begin to suck. Do not give the food too quickly. If a teat is used make several small holes in it instead of one.

As soon as the puppy is three weeks old it can start to learn to lap, and a little Farex mixture can be given with some sugar added. The food should always be made up freshly before each meal. Many breeders start the puppies off with raw meat put twice through the mincer at two and half weeks or as soon as the teeth appear. Give one teaspoonful a day, and gradually increase until at five weeks the puppies are taking two teaspoonfuls a day. Make the mixture in a cup, and stand the cup in a small bowl or saucepan of boiling water, to warm it up to blood temperature.

TUBE FEEDING. There is no doubt that the simplest, quickest and safest method of handrearing a number of puppies is to feed them all by tube. This perhaps sounds frightening to the novice, but if a vet would show the procedure required for inserting the tube down a puppy's throat, and how to test that the tube is in the correct place and not down the air passages, then there is no quicker or safer method. See Dogs and How to Breed Them.

Tube feeding is excellent with very weak puppies who are unable to suck, as no effort is required on their part. Breeders quickly become expert at tube feeding, and a litter of eight puppies can be dealt with in quarter of an hour. If they can manage on six-hourly feeds, the hand-rearing of a litter of eight can be dealt with in a total of one hour a day. Start the first feed at 6 a.m., 12 noon, 6 p.m. and midnight would probably be quite adequate. Premature puppies may require feeding two-to three-hourly.

TO CLEAN THE PUPPY. It is important to top and tail the puppy after feeding it. Take some cotton-wool and wipe the puppy's tummy. This takes the place of the bitch licking its tummy. To enable the puppy to urinate and defaecate, stroke it from its tail end towards its navel, and the puppy will then urinate and defaecate. If the skin looks dry or chapped, place a tiny dab of Nivea cream over the area. Do not do this too frequently, as it may make the skin soft. If at any time the skin by the anus should become sore and red, place a little tannic jelly on the area. This will prevent the puppy wetting the skin there and it will heal under the jelly.

FOSTER-MOTHER. The best thing to be done for the puppies if a real foster-mother cannot be found is to persuade an old brood bitch to take them on. In this case she will often not only clean the puppies up for you after each meal, which is a great time-saver, but take them over and love them altogether; and it has even been known for a very aged bitch of nine years, unmated, to produce milk of her own and to feed the puppies for some of the meals during the day.

If the puppies are to be put to a foster-mother, great care must be taken that she is really going to accept them. Often a bitch has seemed to have accepted puppies, and then later she has turned on them and killed them. So a foster-mother needs watching carefully for a day or two. If she has other puppies, take one of these and rub its tummy over the whole of each orphan puppy, so that it smells of the other one. If there is any stool from one of the foster-mother's own puppies, rub that over the newcomers. If not, place a little of the bitch's milk on the puppies, give them to the bitch quietly and watch her. As soon as she has decided to accept them she will start to lick them. When all seems well, place each puppy on to a teat and then watch the entire feed.

There is no doubt at all that the best solution for the rearing of orphan puppies is to find a good foster-mother. If a large litter of Dobermanns is expected, it is quite a good idea to arrange for a foster-mother in advance, who will take on half the litter.

DEATH OF PUPPIES

If all her puppies should die, the bitch must be kept away from other bitches with puppies and also from all puppies. If the puppies have not suckled from her, there will be no need for treatment to stop her milk, although her fluids should be restricted. If the puppies should die a few days later, the vet will give the dam injections or pills to stop her milk. Always keep an eye on her teats to see that they are not inflamed and that there are no blind teats.

There is a condition of young puppies who are dying which is known amongst breeders as 'fading puppies'. There are a number of causes of this but it is usually an infection. Formerly, the illness was described as being caused by acid milk, but then all milk is slightly acid. These puppies are born healthy and strong, and a few hours or days later they begin to whimper and cry. They have difficulty in sucking and go blue round the mouth, the crying becomes pathetically incessant and they gradually become weaker and weaker until they die. The mother will generally ignore them and put them in a corner.

One of the causes of this illness is haemolytic streptococcal infection. It is thought to infect the puppies before birth; penicillin cures some of these puppies. Gametine serum helps in other cases. B- and E-coli are probably another cause, and occasionally puppies must be taken from the bitch immediately and not be allowed to suck her milk. The puppies can be fed on whipped yogurt for three days until they cease to cry. Then diluted milk mixture can be given. The bitch is usually given chloromycetin injections, and on the third day the puppies may be given back to her. At future pregnancies the bitch should be injected with chloromycetin three or four days before the birth of the puppies, and this usually prevents any recurrence of the trouble. But for all these cases the vet is the only person to advise on the course of treatment.

CAESARIAN SECTION

Some bitches have to undergo caesarian section for one of a number of reasons, but in these days of excellent anaesthetics, such as Fluothane (an I.C.I. product), there is very little danger of the bitch and puppies not surviving. The bitch is generally conscious just after the last stitch is put in, and a few hours later she can be let out to relieve herself. She should not be encouraged to run about, or jump into her box, or take violent exercise. Get the vet to rub the puppies over with a placenta, so that when she comes round she will accept them naturally. It is quite a good idea to keep a couple of placentas to give the bitch to eat when she comes round. The bitch will need only fluids for the first few days.

REMOVING THE DEW-CLAWS

When the puppies are three or four days old they should have their dew-claws cut off. This sounds cruel, but in actual fact the puppies hardly notice it if it is done correctly. If it is the first time that you have done this, get your vet to show you how to do it. The best way is to use a pair of blunt-ended, curved surgical scissors. Get someone to hold the puppy just after it has had a good meal, so that it is contentedly soporific. Start with the dew-claws on the hind legs if there are any, and then do the ones on the forelegs. Get the helper to press the leg for a few seconds just above the little dew-claw, and this will stop the blood supply. Take the scissors and hook them beneath the little pad, lifting the claw with the left hand—but be sure to get the scissors at the very base of the claw. The pressure should be continued just above the claw, then cut sharply and quickly. Place a little powdered potassium permanganate on to the wound and press it in so that it clots. This will prevent any haemorrhage. Repeat for the other foreleg. Keep an eye on the puppy for a few minutes, to make sure that all is well, and then give it back to the dam.

It is kinder not to cut the dew-claws when the dam is in the room, because if the puppy should give a little cry it will naturally distress the dam. Do the operation over a piece of newspaper, as permanganate of potash can stain if it gets wet. If the claw is not cut away deeply enough, it will grow in again and will probably be deformed; in which case, when the puppy is older, the vet will remove it and have to put a small stitch in. At the same time as the dew-claws are being done, the puppies should have their nails cut. The nails become curved and are extremely sharp, and if the puppies are vigorous they can scratch the bitch. The nails should at first be cut once a week and then once a fortnight, and then they should be done as a routine once a month, if necessary.

TAIL DOCKING

This is a barbaric operation which is performed on unfortunate puppies in certain breeds for show purposes only. The removal of a dog's tail, which was given him to wag when pleased, is a sad reflection on civilized people. The removal of the tail in no way benefits the dog. Breeders who have docked hundreds of tails all say that the puppy hardly feels it, but this is not the point. It is *wrong* for a human to mutilate a beautiful dog for such a paltry reason as a show. The docking of horses' tails was abolished more than forty years ago, and it is high time that the docking of dogs' tails was stopped too, and surely it will be in the not too distant future. Future generations will look back in horror at this unnecessary cruelty.

Since, at the moment, it must be done, it is best to get the vet to perform the operation when the puppy is four days old. Sterile scissors (boiled for at least three minutes) should be used. The skin is pulled back and the tail is cut at the first or second joint. The skin is then pulled forward forming a flap which soon heals.

There is another barbaric method for docking tails which is used frequently by breeders. It is probably less cruel than cutting the tail. Pull the skin back, and slide an elastic band off the end of a small tube into which the tail has been inserted as far as the second joint; or, an eleastic band can be wound round the tail and knotted. This cuts off the blood supply and the unwanted part of the tail eventually sloughs off after a few days. This method is less likely to cause infection and there is no loss of blood.

EAR CROPPING

This is an even more barbaric operation than tail docking, but it is not permitted in Great Britain. It was abolished by the Kennel Club, on July 1, 1903. It is performed under an anaesthetic by a vet. The ears are cut round the base to a point at the tip and protected by taping, and are then racked until they have healed.

WORMING

This should be done without fail when the puppies are five weeks old, since after this time the larvae start on their normal migration round the body before returning to the intestines to become adult, and they then lay their eggs. It is vitally important to stop this, especially in the bitches, because once the larvae get into the body and uterus, where they may lodge, it is impossible ever to get rid of them afterwards and the bitch becomes a carrier. Although worming the bitch will get rid of the worms, the larvae will remain in the body.

The vet will give you the correct worm powder. It must be remembered, of course, that a bitch can become re-infested at any time. Symptoms that the puppies have worms may be that they become thin and pot-bellied, and that the skin becomes dry and scurfy. The puppies may have intermittent diarrhoea and occasionally fits. There are two kinds of worm which generally infest dogs. As a rule, it is the roundworm which is found in puppies and the tapeworm which infects the older dog. Worms are usually transmitted to dogs by fleas, and these are often brought by rats and hedgehogs, etc. It is, therefore, most important to keep dogs free from fleas.

Tapeworms in their cystic form can be transmitted from dogs to humans, but they are easily got rid of, one dose of the correct worm powder being sufficient. Tapeworms are easily recognizable, as they look like segments of rice in the stools. Roundworms look like long, thin, white worms.

Before giving a worm powder, the puppy or dog must be weighed accurately. It is imperative that the absolutely correct dosage should be administered. Worm powders are poisonous, and since they are strong enough to kill the worms an overdose by a careless breeder could kill a small puppy. It is wise when giving a worm powder to have someone else to check up on the weight of the puppy and the dosage being given. The powders generally come in pill form, one pill being large enough to dose a 10-lb. dog. Cut a pill into the size necessary to dose the puppy. The easiest way to administer the pill is to put it directly at the back of the puppy's throat, so that he swallows it in one. If, however, the pill disintegrates on cutting, place it between a piece of folded paper and put a rolling-pin over it, or crush the pill between two teaspoons. Place the resultant powder in a fold of the paper, make it into an oblong shape, and divide it up into the fractions required. Never worm a puppy if it has a temperature, or if it seems for any reason off colour.

There was a scare some time ago concerning the dangers of the tapeworm to human beings, and it was related how some children became blind. This is possible, and so it is important that dogs should never be allowed to lick a human's face or mouth. If children come in contact with the faeces of a dog and they then touch their mouth, they could become infested. It is important that all dog excreta should be cleared up daily and not be allowed to lie about on the grass.

Worm eggs probably enter a human being through the mouth, and they immediately make for the intestines. Shortly afterwards they hatch and the worms start on their migration round the body; but, finding themselves in the wrong host, they cannot complete their normal development and they die, and where they die a small cyst forms. Should the cyst be in the eye, blindness could result; but this, luckily, is extremely rare.

WEANING

At about two and a half weeks old, puppies will eat very finely pounded or twice-minced meat, either raw or cooked. The added meals should be increased slowly until five meals a day are being taken by the time the puppies are five weeks old. They can then have three meat meals and two milk and Farex meals a day.

Puppies should learn to eat naturally from a bowl and should not have food thrust into their mouths. One teaspoonful of Collo-Cal D can be given at five weeks, and a pinch of iodized salt.

The dam should be separated from the puppies for longer and longer periods each day after the age of four weeks. By the time the puppies are five or six weeks old they should sleep with the bitch only at night. The longer the puppies feed from the dam, however, the longer they will have immunity from her milk; but the length of time that the puppies are left with the dam depends on how many there are in the litter and how fat and fit the dam remains, or how soon she is tired of them.

Puppies may get diarrhoea with a change of diet or from an infection. One of the best things a puppy should then be given is as much Yogurt as it can take. Sickly puppies may have this beaten up and fed by tube.

CHAPTER 6

THE STUD DOG, ITS IMPORTANCE AND MATING

It is always a problem for a new breeder to decide whether to keep a stud dog or to go out to stud. Stud fees for a really good stud dog are never cheap. If four or five bitches are kept, the cost of stud fees may mount up, but on the other hand the cost of keeping a stud dog in good condition is much more expensive. One thing is certain: unless a breeder can afford to buy a first-class stud dog who has proved himself and regularly begets good puppies, both physically and temperamentally, it is wiser by far not to keep a stud at all. It is then possible to go out to different studs of the correct line for the bitches kept, improving on the breeding of each generation and experimenting with the various stud dogs used. The temptation to use your own mediocre stud dog because he is there, and to use him to all your bitches for convenience's sake, is unlikely indeed to result in the breeding of first class stock, but this depends on how good the stud dog is.

Dobermanns are generally easy to mate provided that the correct days are chosen for the matings. With the aid of two or, if necessary, three people, a little patience and some common sense, failures should not occur.

The choice of a stud dog for any particular bitch should be given much thought, and as much knowledge as possible should be collected. The stud dog must be of excellent temperament, and with no viciousness or nervousness in his breeding. He should be intelligent and have excellent natural working qualities, and be sound both in wind and limb. A good sire commands a high stud fee, usually ranging from £15 to £25. Few good sires can be found whose fee is under £15.

It is extremely important that the stud dog chosen should have been well line-bred, preferably to well-known winning stock. It by no means follows that champions are necessarily the best sires. If you look around and see some typical, sound stock being produced by a particular dog of a suitable blood line, use that stud dog. Do not be tempted to use the dog's litter brother because the fee is less, because the brother will have a totally different genetic make up and may not sire good stock at all. The stud dog chosen should be of the same line or strain as the bitch. Two Dobermanns with the same fault should not be mated together, nor should two dogs with bad temperaments.

The improvement of this magnificent breed rests with the modern Dobermann breeders, and especially with those who are the novices and small breeders of today. Some of you who can stay the course, which is hard, tough and expensive, will be the top breeders of tomorrow.

If, however, a breeder is intending to breed seriously right from the start, it is a good idea to buy a really outstanding, virile stud dog, who is a keen stud, and preferably one who has sired some first-class stock. It is of the utmost importance that the dog should have an excellent temperament and no bad hereditary faults. This type of dog will not be cheap, but if he is a really good sire the breeder will probably get his money back in time from stud fees. Human nature being what it is, it is necessary for a good stud to be seen winning in the ring. There are too many breeders who mate all their bitches to the latest champions, regardless of whether they are suitable in temperament and blood lines for their bitches. This is often done because it is easier to sell puppies by champions for a good price.

A stud dog can normally be used at stud for the first time when he is about ten months old. He should then not be used at stud again until he is about a year old, and by the time he is fourteen months, provided that he is keen, he can have regular stud work. Stud dogs usually produce their best offspring between the ages of three and a half and four years. A stud dog can be used two or three times a week for a month, but he should then be rested. A stud dog requires plenty of nourishing food and extra protein. He should be well muscled up and in good, hard condition. After the age of seven years stud dogs are sometimes less keen on stud work than previously; but most are keen and quick until their dying day.

MATING

The first mating is very important, and the wise breeder will use a young stud dog to an experienced bitch in his own kennel. The dog at this mating should learn to be guided and handled and helped by his owner or handler. This is especially useful if he is a good stud, because when he encounters a difficult bitch he will refuse help unless he has been taught to accept it, and a mating may well be missed, to the frustration of all concerned.

Although the mating of animals is a natural instinct, it is nevertheless not wise to let a stud dog and bitch mate alone, either turned out in a field or in a stable. Two strange dogs put out together might well start a fight, with serious damage resulting to both. Also, if they are uninterested in each other, it would be difficult to know whether a mating had in fact taken place. Even if a mating resulted, during the tie one or both dogs might become over-excited and serious damage could be caused to both during the time.

The easiest way to mate Dobermanns is to arrange to have two or three people to help, and a suitable area should be chosen, preferably in a quiet, cool place, where the two can meet for the first time. The bitch should be wearing a really well-fitting leather collar, and, as a precaution, it is wise to tape her muzzle, attaching the ends of the tape to the collar. It is quite a good idea to attach a short leash to the collar, and the bitch should have a small lump of odourless Vaseline inserted into the vagina. If the bitch has not been mated previously, it might be as well to ascertain that there is no stricture.

The owner or handler of the bitch should hold her securely on both sides of the collar. The owner of the stud dog should then lead in the dog on a leather leash 5–6 feet in length attached to his leather collar. (Never mate dogs wearing chain slip-collars.) The third person (if there is one) should stand a little away from the bitch's rear, so that he can pass on information to the two handlers. The stud dog should be allowed to go up to the bitch and should be permitted to smell her and indulge in a natural courtship, as well as get used to the handlers. The whole procedure should be taken quietly and naturally, and talking should be kept to a minimum. As soon as the stud dog wishes to mount the bitch the third helper should be prepared to steady her, if this is required, or to prevent her from squatting on her haunches, either by holding her up underneath or by supporting her with a knee. Occasionally, the stud dog may become highly excited, in which case he invariably wastes his efforts. If this happens, the third person should motion the stud handler to move the stud away from the bitch, so that he can relax a minute or two before starting again. The third person can be extremely useful, as he can very often assist the stud dog's entry into the vagina at the crucial moment. Care should be taken to see that the stud dog does not rake the bitch with his fore claws, as he would hurt her and leave scars.

As soon as the tie takes place and the stud dog becomes restless, the dogs should be turned. This is done by lifting the stud dog's near-side hind leg over the bitch's back so that the dogs are then standing back to back with their hind legs together. Both the dogs must be held firmly by their handlers. The tie lasts anything from ten to thirty minutes. Occasionally it is less and sometimes a great deal longer. The third person at this stage can fetch two stools or two chairs for the convenience of the handlers, as it can be a tiring business waiting for the tie to finish. During this interval the third person generally goes off to prepare lunch or coffee or a good strong drink for the handlers.

It is important that the uninterested dog should not be hurried, and sometimes he will be encouraged if the bitch is moved away from him, or even if he is taken away from the premises for five minutes or so and then brought back again. He should certainly not be permitted to try to mate the bitch over too long a period, as he will only wear himself out and will become bored.

If a stud dog is really not interested, it is just possible that the bitch is not ready or is over. It is wise for difficult bitches to have the fertility test, so that the correct day may be known. It is surprising how a bitch who has perhaps mated the same stud dog previously will suddenly become most unco-operative and behave in a wild manner at the next mating. Although one mating is generally considered sufficient, there is no doubt that it is safer to have two matings with one day in between, and this certainly seems to leave the stud dog more satisfied.

After the mating the bitch should be shut up quietly in her own quarters for a few hours. The stud dog should also be put away quietly in his own quarters and should on no account be returned amongst his kennel mates for several hours, particularly if there are other stud dogs or male puppies in the area, as a nasty fight could ensue owing to jealousy from the other dogs.

STUD FEES

Stud fees should always be sent with a visiting bitch, or paid when a receipt is given with the pedigree of the dog immediately after the mating. Occasionally, a breeder will accept a puppy in lieu of a stud fee, in which case the owner of the stud dog can register it under his own prefix. But it is always better for a fee to be paid, as the puppy is generally more valuable than the fee. In the event of no puppies resulting from the service, most breeders will give a free service to the same bitch when she next comes into season. The owner of the bitch should inform the owner of the stud dog of the result of the litter; or if there is no litter, then this information should be given a week after the expected date of the arrival of the puppies.

A record of the stud service should be kept in a stud service receipt book, which can be obtained from one of the dog papers. This should include the name of the bitch, her sire and dam, the address and telephone number of her owner, and details of the resulting litter should be added when known.

A good stud dog should be advertised, with mention of his winning progeny. It is from this that he will get used at stud, as well as from his own wins at championship and obedience shows.

CHAPTER 7

GENERAL CARE AND MANAGEMENT

DOBERMANNS are extremely easy to keep in good hard condition, with comparatively little time spent on the actual grooming except before showing. Good feeding, adequate housing and at least two to three miles' exercise a day are essential. Dobermanns are extremely hardy provided that they are well looked after, and they do not normally require much veterinary assistance.

GROOMING

COAT. Dobermanns change their coats twice a year, in the spring and autumn. Before the coat starts to come out the old skin is shed, and this is often seen in the form of scurf. When this happens it is important to brush the hair right down to the roots the way the hair grows, so that the skin is stimulated and left clear and clean and free of the old discarded skin. If scurf continues, stop brushing with a brush and just use a cloth.

BRUSHING. The Dobermann can be given a good vigorous brushing daily and grooming once a week; this is normally found to be quite adequate. The most suitable brushes are either a Mason and Pearson or a curved Addis. The brushing should be followed by a little hand massage to the skin to keep it loose and supple. If the coat looks dry, a little Silvikrin oil hair-dressing can be rubbed on the hands and then gently rubbed over the coat. A good sheen will be obtained if the coat is finally rubbed over with a silk handkerchief or a velvet pad. If there are any bald patches caused by pressure at the elbows, or elsewhere, these can be gently massaged with a little benzyl benzoate emulsion, which keeps the skin soft and enables the hair to grow through quickly.

EYES. Dobermanns do not require much attention to their eyes. The eyes should be bathed in normal saline or weak boracic lotion only when necessary. If the hair around the eyes becomes clogged, a little dry boracic powder rubbed over the area will remove the stain and crust, and the eye rims can then be rubbed round gently with a little cotton-wool moistened with olive oil. If the eyes should ever become inflamed, the vet should be consulted immediately.

EARS. All breeds with pendulous ears are apt to be susceptible to ear troubles, but, provided that they are attended to regularly and a few precautions taken, the ears should give no trouble.

EAR CLEANING. Occasionally, the inside of the ears may become dirty and clogged, in which case the ears require cleaning. It is best to have two people for this, one to hold the dog and the other to clean the ear out with a piece of cotton-wool twisted round the end of a pencil. Pull the ear straight up and twist the cotton-wool into the ear canal, but on no account dig down farther than you can see. If the ears look dirty, the cotton-wool can be moistened with a little olive oil, after which the interior of the ear should be dusted with one part boracic to one part flowers of sulphur. If the ears crackle when pressed at the base, the dog should be seen by the vet.

Never allow the ears to become hard and crusty round the edges. This is apt to happen in the summer months if the dogs are neglected. If the ears should look dry or sore, place a very little Nivea cream or coconut-oil on the edge and shampoo a few days later.

BATHING. Bathing is seldom necessary except under exceptional circumstances and a good walk in a heavy shower of rain will probably clean the dog as well as anything. A dirty dog can be cleaned on a warm, sunny day with Cooper's dressing, which is mixed with water and sponged over the coat and allowed to dry without towelling. If, however, a dog really requires bathing, it can be done once or twice a year. Most breeders find it easiest to bath a dog outside a kitchen window where a spray with a mixer attachment can be fixed to the sink taps. There are many excellent shampoos on the market and all are suitable for Dobermanns. If a Dobermann should happen to roll in something objectionable, the best way to allay the smell until there is time to bath the dog is to rub on a little tomato sauce. It is surprising

how much this helps. Paint or tar can be removed from the coat
with olive oil or butter.

FLEAS. Fleas can be caught from grass in the country, especially where there are rats and hedgehogs about, as such animals
are always infested with these parasites. Dusting the coat with
flea powder will soon rid the dogs of any fleas they may pick up.
As mentioned before, fleas are dangerous as they can cause
worms in dogs. There are special shampoos, which can be
obtained from the vet, which will give dogs protection from
fleas, etc., for about six weeks. These shampoos are not suitable
for young puppies as they are too strong. Anything which is
strong enough to kill fleas, whether by airsprays or powders,
etc., contains poison, and this cannot be good for very young
puppies.

NAIL TRIMMING. Dobermanns do not require to have their nails
cut or filed frequently, particularly if their feet are well knuckled
up as they should be. However, the nails should be looked at
once a month as some dogs' nails grow faster than others; but
many dogs will wear their nails down themselves and keep them
trim. If they are permitted to grow too long, they can prevent the
dogs from walking and galloping in comfort. On the other hand,
the nails should never be cut too short so that they stick up.
Young puppies frequently require their nails cutting or filing as
much as once a week. Occasionally, dew-claws may have been
left on, and these must not be forgotten when cutting the nails, as
they can grow into a complete circle and pierce the skin if they
are neglected.

The best method is to prevent the dogs from seeing the nails
actually being cut or filed. It takes two people to cut or file the
nails: one to hold the dog and distract his attention with a bone
or biscuit, talking to him all the time and shielding his face, and
the other actually to cut or file the nails. Use good nail-clippers,
or a good file, and cut or file the nails at the end of the cuticle.
The cuticle can be seen easily in dogs with light-coloured nails,
but sometimes it can be very difficult to see where to cut with
black-nailed dogs.

When dogs are tense, their nails protrude and look longer than
they normally do, so that great care must be taken not to cut

them too short. Never cut the quick, as this can be very painful for the dog. Should the quick accidentally be cut, it will bleed profusely. Apply immediately some powdered potassium permanganate, which should be kept at hand as a precaution when nails are being cut. This will form a crust and will prevent the nails from bleeding. Afterwards, keep the dog in a pen to prevent him from walking about for a day, until the quick has healed.

SLEEPING QUARTERS

Where the Dobermann is to sleep is often a problem for the new owner. If the Dobermann has his way, he will probably sleep on your bed or in a box by your bed or in an old armchair, and these are not bad ideas if he is the only one and a pet. But show, working and guard dogs are best kept in dry, draught-proof sleeping quarters, although they should all have turns in the house with human companionship during the day.

It is better to keep dogs which live in outside kennels on cedar shavings, sacking or wood wool. The latter can be obtained from Sanibed, Abbotswood, and the second quality is best for dogs. It costs only a few pounds a bale and a little extra if wrapped. If clean, wheat straw can be obtained, this is also good, unfortunately, most straw contains parasites and is better avoided. Sawdust is excellent for mopping up the area where the dogs have relieved themselves, and a good disinfectant should be used to clean the runs and kennels.

THE DOG-RUN

It is not generally wise to allow a Dobermann to run free. A five-foot chain-link fence is generally adequate, particularly one without a top rail, as then there is nothing for the dog to aim at if he tries to jump over the top. A run should not be less than 10 feet by 20 feet, but 20 feet by 40 feet is better. Part of the run should be under cover in case of rain or too hot a sun. The gate must be secured with a strong latch. A cement floor is the easiest to keep clean, although it is apt to harbour worm eggs, and in wet weather it is always damp. Breeze blocks are better as they dry quickly, but they are more difficult to clean, and once a year they should be disinfected with powdered lime and the run left empty for a week.

The actual dog house should be large enough and high enough for the dog, and for the kennel to be cleaned easily. A kennel 4 feet by 6 feet, with the woodwork protected with sheet metal, is an excellent investment. The bed should be 3 feet by 4 feet, and raised at least 6 inches off the ground to avoid draughts, and the sides should be 12-18 inches high. The bedding can consist of sacking filled with clean wheat straw. Dogs require to lie on something reasonably soft, as, owing to their weight, the pressure areas may become bald, particularly the elbows and hocks.

There is one problem which occurs in every household where there are young dogs, and that is the accident on the carpet. The urine of a dog stains a carpet, particularly a plain one, very easily, and the smell of stale urine is most offensive. The most effective way to combat this is to keep a siphon of soda water always at hand. The urine puddle must be mopped up and sprayed immediately. The soda water will prevent staining, but it is no use if the wet patch has been lying there for some time and has dried. A carpet cleaner like a Bex Bissell, with 1001 and a little disinfectant added, is the next best cleaner, but it will not remove an old stain.

GENERAL

Most breeders keep their Dobermanns in outdoor kennels, and generally they do not require artificial heat. However, if lighting and perhaps heating are installed, they should be put in by an expert. In this case it is well worth installing a thermostat at the same time, in order to keep the kennels adequately warm in exceptionally cold weather. The best people to do this are probably the local Electricity Board, who will give an estimate beforehand. Too many fires in kennels are caused by wiring put in by inefficient, do-it-yourself-method handymen. Always keep a fire extinguisher in the kennel, and, if possible, have the room lined with asbestos. Oil stoves should be used with care. Standing one in an old metal dustbin is a good precaution against an obstreperous puppy knocking the stove over and causing a fire.

All excreta should be cleared up in the garden or dog-run as it occurs. It is quite a good idea to use a thick plastic sheet in a corner of the lawn or run. For males, stand an old tin in the centre as a post. The dogs quickly learn to use this area and it can easily be hosed down when necessary. It also prevents the dogs from making ugly yellow patches on the lawn from their urine. If any of the grass withers, water it with a little detergent in the watering-can, as the bubbles help to keep the area wet for a longer period and the grass then grows in quickly.

If a breeder has to keep dogs in permanent runs, it is better to have the area laid out with breeze blocks on 3 inches of sand, as this makes it easier to drain. Once a year the blocks can be watered with weed killer. If there should be an infection in a kennel at any time, small grass runs can be very difficult to disinfect, as the area can harbour germs for a considerable period; and there is also the added work of keeping the grass cut.

All Dobermann owners are wise to take out an all-risks insurance policy for their dogs. The premium is reasonable and the cover gives protection against accident caused by one of their dogs.

CARE OF THE ILL DOBERMANN

Any dog which is looking in the least off colour should be treated as if it had an infectious disease, and it should therefore be segregated from the others immediately as a precaution and the vet consulted. Put the dog in a quiet room with a dim light, and keep him warm and free from draughts. Have a fresh bowl of water by his side and, provided that he has no diarrhoea, feed him on Complan, but never force-feed a sick dog. If he is very ill, he will generally take food off a finger rather than out of a bowl. Little and often is the best way to feed. Starvation for a few days is one of nature's ways of healing.

Keep the dog's mouth clean with a little borax and lemon, and be sure to keep his rear parts clean and dry. Take his temperature in the rectum with a blunt-ended thermometer and keep it there for at least two minutes. Record the reading and write down all the symptoms in a notebook as you notice them. Turn the dog from side to side every two hours to prevent pneumonia. All medicines and injections must be given at the exact times specified by the vet. It will never hurt a dog to go without food for a few days if he is running a temperature, but it is essential that he should have plenty to drink, as he must on no account be permitted to become dehydrated. If the vet agrees, white of egg and a few drops of brandy are excellent and can be given two-hourly, provided that they are not continued for too long. Yogurt is an excellent food and may be whipped up and fed by tube.

If a dog is very ill he may need help to urinate and defaecate, as he may be too weak to stand. This should be done every four hours. He requires brushing daily, as this in itself is stimulating and refreshing. Always talk in a quiet, loving, and gentle voice, and reassure him that he will soon be better. Keep him very quiet and allow him to sleep as much as possible. Try not to pass on your misery and worry to your dog.

THE OLD-AGE PENSIONERS

Old Dobermanns may suffer from rheumatism, failing sight and hearing. They should not be allowed to become too fat and meals should perhaps be given more frequently and in smaller quantities. Guard against toothache. If a dog finds that drinking cold water is painful, get the offending teeth removed. Symptoms should be treated as they arise by the vet. Aspirin helps rheumatism, as does wearing a copper bracelet round the affected joint. Never allow an old dog's feelings to be hurt by the arrival of a new, young, boisterous puppy. If he is suffering, it is better and kinder to have him put quietly to sleep.

TEETHING

The first teeth, of which there are twenty-eight, begin to make their appearance when the puppy is about three weeks old. These teeth are known as the milk teeth, and they have normally come through the gums by the age of six weeks. They are usually regular and in the correct scissor-bite position. These milk teeth have roots which gradually become absorbed and they then fall out. These are followed by the permanent teeth, which usually begin to appear between the twelfth and sixteenth week and can be very painful when they are coming through the gums. Some Dobermanns may be slower and may not get their second teeth until a month later. The fact that the milk teeth are in the correct position does not necessarily mean that the second teeth will be correct.

If the eye teeth are slow in coming out, try to get them out by allowing the puppy to play with a piece of sacking, and then hooking a piece of the hessian round one of the loose teeth and giving it a quick jerk. With luck it will come out with no trouble.

If a dog has had distemper while a puppy, his teeth may become mottled, and he often loses these earlier than normally. Curiously enough, dogs which suffer from cavities seldom have sore gums, whilst dogs which suffer from sore gums seldom have cavities. Dobermanns, like all dogs, hate having their teeth attended to. A good diet with plenty of hard things to chew helps to prevent tartar. Tartar should be removed as it forms. With a special instrument give a sharp pull just above the growth of tartar, and the tartar should come away. Care must be taken not to dislodge an old tooth in the process. A tooth covered with tartar is preferable to no tooth. A charcoal pencil will clean off light tartar. Regular brushing with vinegar and water or household salt keeps the teeth clean.

If Dobermanns are to be exported to Europe, it is essential that they should have a full complement of teeth, including six incisors in the upper jaw and six in the lower. In the U.S.A. a jaw which is over $\frac{3}{16}$ inch overshot or more than $\frac{1}{8}$ inch undershot would disqualify a Dobermann. There are two large canine teeth in each jaw and seven molars on each side of the lower jaw, and six on each side of the upper jaw, making a total of forty-two teeth, though some dogs have two extra molars.

CHAPTER 8

REGISTERING, SELLING AND EXPORTING

As soon as puppies are about two months old they should be registered at the Kennel Club. The Kennel Club supply two forms for the registration of puppies: one for one puppy only, the other for more than one puppy of the same litter. These are easily filled in and must be signed and dated and sent to the Kennel Club, 1–4, Clarges Street, Piccadilly, London, W.1. The cost is 50p per puppy. If a puppy has not been registered by the breeder, the registration fee is £1.50. When a registered puppy is sold, the new owner must be given a Kennel Club transfer form, duly signed by the breeder. This should be accompanied by the pedigree (also signed), the inoculation certificate, and a diet sheet.

SELLING

The best age to sell Dobermann puppies, if they are to go as pets, is probably about eight to twelve weeks. If, however, a Dobermann is wanted for show or for breeding purposes, particularly the former, then the purchaser is wiser not to buy one under the age of four or five months. At this age, naturally, a dog will be considerably more expensive, especially if he is really good, because, having kept him so long, the breeder will no doubt be loath to part with such a good dog.

As soon as the puppies are ready for sale, and not before, put some advertisements in the dog papers, the local papers, and perhaps the *Exchange and Mart* or *The Times*. Give full particulars concerning breeding etc., using the name of a famous sire or grandsire, if there is one, or a well-known blood line. Never start an advertisement with 'Superb puppies for sale', especially if they are of only pet quality. Answer all enquiries promptly and efficiently with prices of the dogs for sale, making them subject to being unsold. Never send photographs of dogs if they are required back. They are seldom returned. If you require any-thing to be sent back, such as a copy of the pedigree, send a stamped addressed envelope. For telephone enquiries write down the names of callers and their telephone number, in case you should wish to cancel an appointment or for any other reason.

If there are any puppies for sale, keep a list by the telephone, with the prices. Do not change prices from customer to cus-tomer, as it soon gets round. If you are not sure how much to ask for a puppy, ask the owner of the stud dog used, or some know-ledgeable breeder, who will give you an idea of current prices. When selling a puppy always make out a diet sheet for it, and suggest what it will require to eat when older. Also give some advice on the most common puppy ailment—diarrhoea.

THE PREFIX

All well-known kennels should have a prefix or affix for their dogs. This is really best described as a kind of surname for the dogs in a kennel. The prefix must be applied for to the Kennel Club, and costs £3. A retaining fee of £1 a year must be paid annually, unless otherwise arranged. A prefix can be compound-ed for life for £7. After ten annual payments the compounding fee is £5. The choice of a prefix is extremely important. It should be easily pronounced and reasonably short, so that it can be remem-bered.

The entire name that a dog can be registered with must not contain more than twenty-four letters. A new owner may add, at a cost of £2, his own suffix to a dog, but in this case there may be more than twenty-four letters in the full name. Once a dog is regis-tered its name cannot be changed and no other dog may be given the same name again within less than ten years. A name once entered in Stud Book may never be used again.

If a dog is to be shown before the registration has come through from the Kennel Club, the letters 'NAF' must be written after the name on the entry form. This means 'Name Applied For'. If the dog has changed hands and the tranfer has not yet been confirmed by the Kennel Club, the letters 'TAF' must be written after the name, meaning 'Transfer Applied For'.

EXPORTING

Most breeders take a pride in exporting good dogs to foreign countries, and there is always a certain amount of kudos attached to a kennel that exports good dogs. However tempting the offers might be, there are some countries that it is wiser never to export dogs to, unless they are to be owned by Europeans or Americans or unless the new owner is known personally to the exporter. Moslem countries should be avoided and certain other countries too. It is up to the breeder to make quite sure what sort of a home and people he is exporting his dogs to. This applies to Dobermanns particularly, as they are rather large and new owners may not understand what is entailed in owning a Dobermann. Any dog which is exported should be of a very high standard, and the price should be the price of a good dog at home plus a coverage for all extra cost, time and trouble which goes into the exporting of a dog.

Each country has its own import regulations, and a copy of these can be obtained from the Ministry of Agriculture, Fisheries and Food. The Kennel Club will supply an export pedigree. This is always required and cost £2.50 for all countries except Austria, Australia, Canada, France, Germany and the U.S.A., where additional information is necessary, and the cost for these countries is £5. The dog requires at least three generations of registered breeding. The vendour can sign the transfer certificate on behalf of the purchaser.

If the dog is going to the U.S.A., the new owner must be an American citizen if the dog is to enter duty free. Some countries insist on the registration numbers being included of all dogs shown in the pedigree. All dogs which are exported must also have a health certificate and a certificate regarding monorchidism and cryptorchidism, even though this seldom occurs in Dobermanns. Some countries—for example Sweden and Australia—require blood tests; others, like the Argentine, require passport photographs of the dogs; and there are some countries which have a quarantine period in spite of the dogs coming from Britain. Dogs going to Australia may now fly or go by ship. Also, they may not go direct from the U.S.A. to Australia without undergoing quarantine in Britain first, and then they must go by sea and finally submit to another two-month period of quarantine in Australia.

Some countries insist on an anti-rabies injection. This, of course, is not possible to have done in Britain, as there is no rabies and therefore no anti-rabies vaccine is kept. But all countries accept this for Britain.

Unless the new owner takes the dog with him, exporting it entails a great deal of work and organization. Therefore the gross price of the dog must include the cost of all the additional expenses, such as the freight, box, insurance, export pedigree, delivery charges, port and customs dues, tips, veterinary fees and certificates, injections, blood tests, transfer form, medicine box, etc. The dog box should be clearly labelled several times. Put the dog's name on the top, so that he can be called by it by the staff dealing with him, and also the address and telephone number of the new owner; and make absolutely certain that the box is well secured, but do not lock it. On the handle tie a lead and inside the box place some food and a bone. If possible, write any instructions in the language of the country that the dog is being exported to.

The question of payment is sometimes difficult. It is best, however, made by a banker's draft; and you should never send a dog abroad until you have received full payment—unless, of course, you know the purchaser well.

CHAPTER 9

SHOWING, JUDGING AND CLUBS

THERE IS a great deal more in showing dogs than meets the eye. All judges by no means have the same ideas, so that a dog may win the Challenge Certificate one week and find himself bottom of Open Dog the next. This, of course, is all rather baffling to the novice, but it happens to be part of the dog game. Some people think that it would be rather dull without this element of uncertainty, and to many people it is the constant surprises which are the main fascination. 'Chacun à son goût!'

Preparation for dog shows takes a long time, starting with the early training, and then grooming, etc. There are some dogs which have the natural character and temperament for showing and are show-offs from birth; whilst a much better dog physically, with no show temperament, will often go cardless. Fortunately, Dobermanns are superb dogs to show, as they are so easily trained and they mostly thoroughly enjoy being exhibited.

There is probably nothing more enjoyable than showing a really superb dog that never sets a foot wrong, which is both beautiful and well trained, and which is much admired by the other exhibitors and also the ringside spectators, and is a joy and credit to his owner and breeder.

A show dog should have been taught to move smartly on a lead with his head held well, moving always on the left-hand side of his handler. Every Dobermann is an individual and moves better at certain speeds, and so it is important to find the best speed for your particular dog. The Dobermann must be trained to stand and be examined by a stranger, allowing his mouth to be opened, and having his body, legs and tail gone over. He should always be given great praise when he is good and doing what is required. Before going to a show, the dog should have mixed with different breeds, so that he is not surprised when he first encounters them at a large show. The day before a show a dog

112

should be bathed, if necessary, and brushed well, and his eyes and ears must be cleaned. At the same time his nails should be cut or filed down and his teeth cleaned if dirty. He should also have a routine training the day before the show, especially if he has not been to one for some time.

Advertisements for shows appear in the weekly dog papers. Write to the show secretary concerned for a schedule, if you are not already on his mailing list. The entry forms require careful filling in, but they are quite straightforward. Before being posted they should be checked, preferably by someone else. Do not forget to include the cheque; because if you do, it gives the poor show secretary a considerable amount of extra work.

Keep a special bag for all show requirements. As far as possible, this should be packed after each show ready for the next one, and then only water, food, some bones and the entry cards need to be added the evening before. Newspapers, a disinfected Spontex cloth, blankets, bones, food, water, bowls, kennel cards, titbits, salt biscuits, collars and leashes, brush, entry passes, and a Biro must be included in the travelling kit, and, if the exhibitor is wise, a Thermos flask of strong coffee, a picnic lunch, and, for a headache sufferer, some aspirin.

The Kennel Club do allow kennel cards to be placed on benches. These must only carry the name of the prefix, the owner, the address and the telephone number. They must not measure more than 8 inches by 5 inches. They are best made of plastic which does not bend and is washable. They can be obtained from first class printers in most areas. Hand-outs can be made from the Christmas number advertisement.

Exhibitors should not gossip in the ring and should be on the alert with their dog. They must know his age when asked by the judge, and they must always keep their dog on a short leash and under control. Clothing should be suitable and comfortable, with flat-heeled shoes, and one should have a convenient pocket lined with a small plastic bag for holding titbits for bribing the dog. Have a card clip for the ring number on your lapel, and ascertain the number of your exhibit before getting your number card from the steward.

Never take winning or losing too seriously: there is always

another show and another judge. If you feel that a judge has not been fair to you for any reason, always be sporting, and give him a second chance at another show. It is most important that all exhibitors should show sportsmanship, both when they win and when they lose. In the exhilaration of winning, never forget the bitter disappointment which may be felt by the losers, and there are many of these. Finally, never thank the judge for putting up your dog. He is only doing his job.

JUDGING

There are two types of judge: the all-rounder who judges all breeds, and the specialist who knows perhaps only one or two breeds. Sooner or later most people in a breed are asked to judge. A few will make a good job of it the first time they judge, because they have a natural eye for an animal, the right temperament and a good memory, and because they have a good organizing ability and are never influenced by the other end of the lead. They must have the courage to do what they consider correct, regardless of how unpopular it may be or of what some other judge may have done previously.

A bad judge is thoroughly muddle-headed, nervous, and, although he may have been breeding for thirty years, would not recognize a good dog if he saw one. Naturally, there are judges between these two extremes, who in time will learn what a good dog is and who, with more experience, will be able to assess one dog against another, but this will often be at the expense of the exhibitor. Such individuals are unlikely ever to become really good judges.

On arrival at a show, the judge must report to the secretary's tent or office, to be given a judge's badge and a luncheon voucher. The routine should be discussed with the steward(s). Mark up the judging book with the entries of the dogs in each class. Stewards often kindly do this. On a separate piece of paper, or, better still, in your own notebook, which you keep for judging and use from show to show, rule off six or seven columns, the first for the class and the following spaces for first, second, third, and as many placings as are required. Make a dividing line between the dog classes and the bitch classes. After judging each class, enter up the placings of the exhibits. This will constitute a reference to prevent reversing an order, which is much frowned upon by the Kennel Club. There are, however, occasions when the order has to be reversed, such as if a dog will not move well in a later class.

Notes for the show report should be done with a few easy, shorthand signs, such as four stars if a dog is outstanding and one star if poor, and you should have a sign for a good head, eye, mouth, etc. The colour and sex should also be noted. When writing the report for the dog papers, bear in mind the people who read the report and have not been at the show. Sum up the general appearance of the dog and mention his good points, starting with the head. You are more popular if faults are not mentioned, but this may be got round by saying something to the effect that such and such a dog is 'not as strong in hind movement as the one above'. But a judge is of little value if he reports that all the dogs were good. Novices can learn a great deal from the show reports. It is better to put up a dog with one outstanding fault than a mediocre dog with no particular virtues. Any fool can see a fault, but it takes a clever judge to be able to assess the good points of each dog. Judging should always be done on the good points and never on the faults of a dog alone. Everyone should realize that the perfect dog does not exist in any breed. Do not be over-biased for exaggerated breed points such as the number of teeth. Look for typical, sound dogs with good temperaments.

In the ring the dogs should be lined up, and when all are present take a good look at each dog. Do make them move round the ring in an anti-clockwise direction, as this wakes the dogs up and makes them realize that showing has started. Choose out in your mind which you think are the four or five best dogs. Examine each dog individually. Stand back well away from the dog and study his overall proportions. Then approach the dog slowly, allow him to sniff the back of your hand, and then with gentle but firm movements proceed to examine the dog in detail. Dogs which stand beautifully with correct fronts will often be found to plait when moving. Press the hindquarters firmly to feel the strength of the muscles and joints. Note the expression of the eyes, the size of the ears and their placement, the shape of the skull, and the strength of the lower jaw, and note whether the head resembles a blunt wedge. Then get the handler to move the dog either straight up and down the ring or in a triangle, so that his movement can be observed going away from you, sideways, and coming towards you. Unless there is something noticed during the individual examination which is bad, such as the mouth, you will usually find that the dogs that you noticed first will be the ones that you will finally put up. Do not change the order of the dogs once you have decided on it. You may yourself become muddled and do something perhaps that you did not intend to do.

The top three dogs in open classes are often equally good and could change places if you judged them an hour later. A dog may often just win on showmanship, and every dog, however well trained, will occasionally have his off day. Remember that each class you judge is a senior class to the previous one. The winner of the Open Class is judged with all the unbeaten dogs and with the runner-up, provided that he has not been beaten in a previous class. Watch that all the exhibitors are behaving correctly towards each other, and that no dog is being attracted to the side of the ring by a ringside spectator. Handlers should be penalized if they allow their dogs out on a long leash into the centre of the ring, if they over-extend the hind-legs, and if they over-handle their dogs. After each exhibitor has moved his dog for you, thank him before turning to the next dog. (And while on the subject of thanks, do remember to write to your steward(s) afterwards to thank them for their help.)

Occasionally, after you have finished judging, a few exhibitors may ask you about their dogs, as they genuinely want to learn about their faults and good points. There are some exhibitors who may come up to you very hot under the collar to know why you put their dog down. Perhaps you had placed it higher at a previous show, but at each show the dog is up against a different selection of dogs, and perhaps he was going on grass at one show and on a hard surface at the next. This type of ground variation can make a great deal of difference. Always remain calm and polite, and simply say that you like their dog very much but that you just preferred the one that you placed above it.

CLUBS

The Kennel Club, which was founded in 1873, controls dogdom in Great Britain. All dogs must be registered at the Kennel Club before they may be exhibited at limit, open or championship shows. Only championship show judges have to be approved by the Kennel Club. The Kennel Club has a ladies' branch, and membership of both is severely limited. The Kennel Club publishes the *Kennel Gazette* 25p each month or free for members, and its Stud Book is issued once a year. Both are well worth receiving, and the former is a good place to advertise a kennel.

At the present time there are four breed clubs. The Dobermann Club was the original one and was founded in 1948. The annual club subscription is £1 single or £1.50 joint. A championship show is held every year. The other three breed clubs are the Scottish Dobermann Club, the North of England Dobermann Club and the Midland Dobermann Club.

The addresses of the club secretaries can be obtained from the Kennel Club.

CHAPTER 10

AILMENTS AND USEFUL HINTS

IN A SMALL book of this size it is not possible to write more than a few lines on some of the more common ailments which occasionally befall Dobermanns. There are, however, certain articles that should be kept, including a medicine chest or cupboard specially stocked with canine requirements. An infra-ray lamp is always useful to have, but the following are 'musts': a clinical blunt-ended thermometer, an eye-dropper, curved surgical scissors, nail tweezers, cotton-wool, gauze, Sellotape to be used instead of a bandage, Friar's balsam, potassium permanganate, Brand's Essence, colloidol calcium with vitamin D, cod-liver oil, Complan, Protogest, Dettol, flea powder, worm pills, eye lotion, glucose and vitamins.

ADMINISTERING LIQUID MEDICINES. To administer a liquid is extremely easy with a large breed like the Dobermann. The liquid can be given from a large spoon. The head should be held up and a finger inserted into the corner of the mouth where the lip conveniently tends to hang. Pull out this protruding part of the lip and insert the spoon. The liquid will run into the back of the dog's mouth and he will automatically swallow it provided that his mouth is kept shut until he has done so.

ANAL GLANDS. These are two small glands situated on either side of the anus. If a dog has enough roughage in his diet and adequate exercise, they should never require attention. If they become blocked and swell, take the dog to the vet and he will show you how to express the glands correctly. If this is done badly by an inexperienced person, it can cause the dog much pain and discomfort and can be dangerous.

ARTIFICIAL RESPIRATION. This is done when a dog or puppy, for some reason or other, stops breathing. For Dobermann puppies, the easiest method when they are tiny is to lay the dog out on his back across the palms of your hands, and then quite strongly bring his head and tail together. Open out the hands again so that the dog is lying with his back arched backwards, and then repeat by bringing your hands together again. If the dog is heavy, rest your hands and arms on a table for support. This should be done about twenty times to the minute. A few drops of brandy can be put on the back of the tongue and smelling salts can be placed near the nostrils. Never give an unconscious dog anything by mouth. Mouth-to-mouth and nostril resuscitation combined with rib palpitation can produce excellent results. For an adult Dobermann it is best to lie the dog on its side and to compress the ribs in and out about twenty times a minute. But remember: never give an unconscious dog anything by mouth.

BAD BREATH. This, fortunately, is not common in Dobermanns, but it can be caused by eating raw meat, by a bad tooth, dirty teeth, indigestion, or occasionally by kidney trouble. Charcoal tablets sometimes help: in the case of a bad tooth the removal of the cause should cure the trouble. Amplex tablets are a palliative treatment, but they will not remove the cause.

BURNS AND SCALDS. These are extremely painful for the dog, and often initially there is no evidence to be seen. The dog must first be treated for shock and pain. Give one or two tablets of Codeine or Disprin every four hours. If the skin is entire, apply a thick covering of bicarbonate of soda, and, if possible, bandage or cover the area with gauze, and keep this on with Sellotape. If the burn is small, tannic jelly could be used. If the skin is broken, apply sulphathiazole ointment, as burns become septic very easily. Veterinary advice must be sought immediately. The full extent of the damage will normally not be seen for three weeks, when the hair starts to slough off. The dog requires plenty of fluid, and a rich-protein bodybuilding diet during the three weeks of convalescence.

CONCUSSION. This is a brain injury. Put the dog in a dark room and keep him quiet and reasonably warm. Ice, wrapped in a flannel or a cold compress, can be applied to the back of the head. Get veterinary help immediately and give nothing by mouth if the dog is unconscious. If the breathing is difficult, try artificial respiration gently in the method already described but without moving the dog's head.

DANDRUFF. This is the shedding of dry skin and can be prevented with a good diet and by giving seaweed powder and plenty of green vegetables. Give the dog some good exercise to tone him up. Dettol applied to the skin before bathing will help. Avoid using a hard brush if there is any dandruff and use a chamois leather instead. Linseed oil added to the diet also helps, as does vitamin A.

DIARRHOEA. This is comparatively common in puppies. It can be caused by worms, a chill, an infection, or a B-coli enteritis. Treatment must be immediate, giving kaolin mixture three times a day. The dog must be isolated from the others. Stop all food, especially milk, but give plenty of water. If the diarrhoea continues, give a little arrowroot boiled in water. A little Protogest may be added, and later also boiled rice. As soon as there has been one day free of diarrhoea start the dog with small quantities of food, but avoid milk for another twenty-four hours. If the diarrhoea seems very loose with a bad smell, send for the vet. He will probably give a kaolin mixture with an antibiotic added, such as streptomycin.

If the diarrhoea still continues, a change of antibiotic, such as aureomycin or neomycetin, etc., will be tried. Never use a stronger antibiotic or medicine than necessary. If there should at any time be blood and mucus in the stools, this can be extremely serious, and the dog must have an antibiotic injection immediately—by which I mean within an hour of seeing the blood. Dogs have been known to die of this within a few hours. Therefore, if it occurs late at night, never decide to wait until the morning. It may be too late then to save your dog.

Care must be taken that the dog does not become dehydrated, and so plenty of liquids should be given. White of egg whipped up with a little brandy can be given hourly to a very sick dog. In case there is an infection, it is important to clear up any diarrhoea as it occurs, and to keep the dog segregated on warm, clean bedding.

DISTEMPER AND INFECTIOUS HEPATITIS. These are highly infectious diseases. Distemper infects the central nervous system and hepatitis the liver. There are over fifty kinds of distemper virus. There is no known cure for virus infections, so that the symptoms must be treated as they appear. With distemper there is usually fever, discharge from the eyes and nose, vomiting, and later there may be diarrhoea with complications of pneumonia. Dogs often seem to recover at this stage, but the virus has not finished its course of destruction on the central nervous system, and the most dangerous period then follows.

If the brain becomes damaged, fits may result or even death. Some dogs may be left with twitching of the limbs, called chorea, which can continue all their lives, although cases have been known to cure themselves up to six years old. We had a Labrador who stopped twitching five years after a distemper infection.

DOG BITES. These should be attended to by the vet, as they can go septic very quickly. The dog requires an immediate antibiotic injection, and the wound should be kept open by fomentations for a week and should not be premitted to heal earlier. Penicillin generally stops any infection.

ECLAMPSIA. This is caused by lack of calcium in the brood bitch. The bitch has a type of convulsion. It very rarely occurs, however, in maiden bitches. The convulsions generally occur during whelping or about the third week after, and eclampsia is more likely to occur if there is a larger litter. Bitches should be given a course of colloidol calcium with vitamin D, which the vet will prescribe, for the week before whelping; and Stress should be added to the diet during the last month.

The first indication that a bitch may be having eclampsia is the alteration of temperament. The bitch becomes hysterical and then lethargic, convulsions may follow, and she can even become unconscious. The vet must be sent for immediately. Remove the puppies, and they must not be permitted to feed from the bitch until she has quite recovered. The vet will inject large quantities of calcium, and will also give the bitch a strong sedative. She should be kept very quiet in a darkened room and touched as little as possible, and only very gently and quietly when it is essential. Some vets will give a bitch which has suffered from eclampsia previously a course of parathyroid tablets ten or twelve days before whelping is due. In some cases this seems to be effective. The bitch should be on no account be mated at her next season.

EYE ULCERS. This complaint is not common in Dobermanns, but it can be caused by a knock or a scratch on the eyeball, probably when playing with other dogs; or it can also be caused by an infection. The first sign is a blue film over the eye. The vet should see the eye immediately and will probably prescribe cortisone drops such as Betsolan. Provided that there is no infection, I find that putting the drops in hourly for three days usually clears the film quickly. The drops should be put into the inside corner of the eye. If they are dropped into the centre they roll off.

If, after three days, the eye is not cured, change to another medicine such as Terra-Cotril ointment, but your vet will prescribe what is necessary. A course of cod-liver oil daily helps. Some ulcers can become very bad, with the eye protruding and yellow, and these are exceedingly painful for the dog. However, it should hardly ever be necessary to remove an eye. After an ulcer the eye always remains scarred.

HEART ATTACK. This may last from a few seconds to five minutes. Lie the dog on his right side, with the head lower than the body. Pull the tongue forward and place a teaspoonful of brandy on the back of it. Use smelling salts, which stimulate a reflex action on the heart and lungs. Get the vet immediately for further treatment. A dog who has suffered a heart attack should lead a very quiet life afterwards.

MANGE. There are two kinds of mange, sarcoptic and demodectic, both of which are highly contagious to dogs and humans. They are caused by two parasites which burrow under the skin. It is extremely unfortunate if a kennel becomes infected by either of these parasites, particularly the demodectic type, which is difficult to eradicate, as the parasite can live dormant in the skin and only reappear if the dogs should at any time become off-colour. Dogs, however, which are well cared for and fed really well will not catch mange easily.

Sarcoptic mange can be cured in ten days with Tetmosol solution, and the vet will tell you what to do. It is possible to tell which mange is which without a skin-scraping test. Dogs must be segregated from each other, and the scabs carefully removed with a little pure Tetmosol as they appear, provided that there are not very many of them, as Tetmosol is highly poisonous. The dogs are given a nine-day treatment. They are washed in Tetmosol solution, covering one-third of the body at a time each day, taking three days to cover the entire body, and being very careful to avoid the eyes. An unsightly bald patch is left where the scabs have been removed.

When the infection has been cured, coconut oil on the area will help to grow in the new hair as quickly as anything, and this will probably take about six weeks. Demodectic or follicular mange is very difficult to cure permanently and it often leaves a thickening of the skin. The bedding and pens where the dogs are kept must be disinfected every day, all bedding and cotton-wool used for removing scabs should be burnt immediately after use, and the dogs should be fed on an extra nourishing diet. Extra care must be taken over the treatment of young puppies. Breeders who are terrified of mange may put on too strong a solution, and puppies have been known to have been killed by the unnecessary cruelty. Nuvan Top is an excellent spray against fleas and parasites and it is also useful against mange. It can only be obtained from a veterinary surgeon.

MÉSALLIANCE. This is the term used for an undesired mating. The bitch must be taken to a vet within twelve hours of the occurrence for a hormone injection. This is nearly always effective, but the bitch cannot be mated again to another dog that season.

STINGS. *Bee stings.* Remove the sting and apply alkaline, such as washing soda, to the area.

Wasp stings. There is no sting to remove. Apply a diluted acid, such as vinegar or lemon juice.

INDEX